THE BRASS SCREW IN THE SHOE

JOHN EMERY MORSE

Paperback: 978-1-965632-27-7
eBook: 978-1-965632-28-4
Library of Congress Control Number: 2024920467

Ordering Information:

Prime Seven Media
518 Landmann St.
Tomah City, WI 54660

Printed in the United States of America

TABLE OF CONTENTS

If I Believe In You I Don't Think I Can Believe In Myself. What's True?

"What is Kow Tow John?" asks Reyna? Is "Why do you think Steve? You are not poetical philosophy nor are you a carpel a stamen of the next generations wheat. What makes the point of gaining or loosing time, personally, for the world, for the nation, flying an airplane a jet, a rocket, something that can lift above the gravity of time? A chronological question of compartments answering a question with a question in this greased axle where the modern day word started like Adam?" "No" says Rey. "Is God and newborn the first word the first thoughts of time"? Reyna says "Your mother said John, if you are a pilot you will only marry your airplane, and you act like you're your own savior with Johnny jet wing walker your lord and god. Where is Maria, where is the virgin, where is Aleysa, even where am I?"

In the forest which has burned and is now in the domain of Michelle burning for a hundred years as the sparks of the Indians hookah vape and remember tobacco as the favor of a toothless Osiris of this nation once Seth's jealousy tore it apart. "Yes Reyna, at this time."

Is there lightning at the top of Jerusalem mountain which doesn't burn except to fry burgers, treeless food from the plains of chaparral Gabriel Abraham house of ceiling to floor glass windows. "Have your visions sleep for awhile how are you to eat with damaged eye teeth." said Reyna. "This home is more healthy than your spirit going over the hill by lightning. And you should not spit. One tooth already has to be fixed so that when you awake you can see again."

Rey sat up aghast and cunningly demanded "Dissolve poetry! Take Pegasi wing off and attach it to your shoulder, take two of his legs and fix your write knee with them. Then stand on one leg."

Then John knew and answered Rey's questions as an Osiris "Maybe you'll find your right hip underneath your armpits. Who do I eat sweet dessert with, as Venus pheromones? My balls of my eyes are tucked in the left side of my head duck webbing to the write side. My right leg tucking what is left of fertility deep into my right groin.. All night I did I did I saw a cat."

"Conquer time eh Rey" said John. "Use your mortar and brick columns of in slavery peace with no heat in the night and if in anger then be determined by brimstone even fir a smoking forest for switching a cat tail to conquer the older men rule of thumb time is not of the essence from thee. You have forever for twenty years you perceive I four months for two unknown. Your church has twice attempted to forsake my squeaky wheel seniority rights by kingdom coming greased axle and after eye first found the beauty by Pantene and wine you supplant Maria and child from Reyna and say once upon a time with Reyna is all I shall receive to restore the fertility orb. And your rights shall be forever in the slavery of servitude whereas I agreed several years ago with a brother that neither of us would be the slaves of each other's time. Maria and child I knew your choice three days before it was made by you. You did not decide in my favor. My keys were again to be principally replaced."

So you sea off with your head as you go to Hawaii and I off with my head as I go to Florida and the dentist. My game is with the poet Pegasus not being in France and Nice. Or was that the niece from the virgin, Reyna which is I John's intention. That said you are in-kin and where are the fathers Maria?

You take for granted my time is your time Rey. You are mean, call people you're working with chicken and live on steak. Burgers are from Willy and he is a Nice man. I live on the sensitivity of Reyna of Japan trying to make apologies to my mother a Youman who tried not successfully to make me into a You-woman because of you Rey. And the Philippines feed me tenderly but darkly a cup of coffee for a breakfast the way of the Cow Tao. I am told this is what happened to the Kung Pao not close in region to Lao tzu of the Tao but with similar harm in servitude from your race Rey which judges by building the heart chest area by filling it out of the clouds of a lion or Saber tooth tiger with chicken.

"Fish for it John. Fish sticks for the pinkies of Kung Pao of Korea. Japan has the silver lining of rain and fire as much and more experienced than "whats" which I call cop law. This is your train and trade of entropy they are 'all time' for the position you have placed me in which is all sergeancy to your Pegasus ideals."

Motion lotion of porcelain water does not make what I see in the windows. Except of your mind, the eyes of the soul. Do you not see destroyed nature and empathy of man turned into pigs blood the concrete of Japan in war. Your I's are like an oath bearer determining the anti-christ with the sensitivity of a skewering sawmill to split splinters of stumps into blood" The flies have been eating breakfast of you Rey, so shall I".

Then that this is good as demanded by Reyna and the virgin, eye shall place a ring around the round table so that blowing in the wind is tied down and mother nature is stabilized. And no flies on you John, Reyna and virgin once the woods have been sprayed.

Then Rey who is really a doctor and papa Rey said "There is a time for lateral motion as the men move in and out and there is a time for vertical motion as all men rise. So eat be merry even with cross Rey in cross merry weather so that you could see the Wave in your rat king of blindness, of surf the Murphy, John the ocean your father and mother loved dearly. The undertow of the ocean pulls only the weak out John you are to balance your strength and sea and see and with happiness Si. Rise John as I pronounce your rights to the promise ring of the virgin secured to the smoking table by the wine bottle of burgers time outback. "And forever do I see, sea, and yes? As long and short of lateral movement of men and women who surf to the vertical rise of eating and writing life from the bottom of my heart."

Should I sit up with my hips or pot, my legs have lost a lot? My head does spin left or right, write and left along with my heart. And I get the notion of the dentists antibiotics that writing is so mechanical and all that's left in the end is art. These are the swirlies John "the motion lotion of porcelain water" and I perceive that Rey's humor of declaring a persona non gratis an Antichrist has diminished to rest and sleep as his poetry is as imperceptible as a fact. Declared mechanical for the swirlies win and potentially for the year of the rat. Ours is not to beat the esteem of Stanley the steamer our brother's chosen grandpa though Turlough grandpa he also be, parked in Jet stream trailer, but to serve with maintenance of each ones soul as that has a will to be. And Reys point "Flies in the bottle, vapes in the tube, I won't get through with you until there is an iv in the boob." John your rights with the Catholic Church are devoid and so are their church rights with your work. You may join the Vietnamese Protestant church and good luck.

Then I had a burg eye experience a hallucination a photo-receptive marketing a dream I was Aladdin thrown into the water saved by the genie and only had Aleysa and held onto Aladdin's Lamp. Then Aleysa had a dream and an angel entered her and said " You will have a son but that seed may or may not come from John but you will have to make love to him to have that child. He will be Aladdin".

So to Africa as it is to be: if a hippo pocket mess has a miss and he puts her preferred munchies in his pocket wallet, an Osiris phallic symbol, and pays for them he has a heterosexual pocket. With this pocket he is a hippo pocket less mess of Michelle's influence. Which be eye and which be time and energy as I go up and stay up. Is the less mess above or in sleep laying down. In my eyes as I wake and see the world or in an inner eye of dream. And the hippies and hippos walk on as there hips do the motor motion that is hopefully of the sedentary and your motor row tore conscious of balance of the surf which is wit to you Rey although of dream you are too burning.

Your mouth in its inquest of anger and snoring is causing the folding of a universe throat the Oedipus Rex or blinding schizophrenia of "Hiding In The Mirror" or "The Physics of Star Trek" folding of the universe around a throat. John. Thus is your psychology and comprehension as empathetic as treating a man like a continually kicked waste basket.

Where am I coming from? Well the birds, the morning sunrise, the zen garden, the haiku, the reward of expression from writing not whittling this thru for construction and real estate. How impractical compared to surfing although Rey you seem to get an unknown faerie load off my back. You talk about the success of surf the June gloom in the uv heat and that is your comparison for the basis of happiness fact.

Life goes on whether in heaven or a choir and there is still satisfaction for medicine and I of neck god and love. Arguing is a speeding anger based on loose and fear of unknown motion lotion falling from high and being confused. Life is getting better it is getting petty in the pelvis overnight with home scheduling and allowance as we both see each other's way.

Almost all the way to the sun in the morning after a cup of stabilizing coffee and Aleysa agrees that empathy should be love not kicking in the waste basket.

Where is the sound and contrast of the house of the neighborhood? Almost and least just mean that we are all sinners. What you can see defines how well the house is kept and how well you can hear defines the court. Time is not completed 100% in this case as the sunrises tomorrow today are also to complete the 100% clarity from the motes in our brain to the sun's promise of " all time". Until at least I return home to contact the house with magna eagle vision which knows what is alive and what is of deadwood.

There should be a son and daughter " making friendship" to the sun's promise of " all time" and God's promise of a living love. Or are we all hiding in the mirror of the house and not speaking our minds without fear of retribution of malice.

Get the situation petty then and know why this daughter Maria loves you sun, son, which I take as meaning more than the word petty of today. Love is more than a pun on the word petty John says Reyna. Is it a living love or a petty one Maria that will hold but lacquer as the sun also rises on Carson St. where John is expected to buy your son a car besides the backyard at Mariposa and Clarion?

I could not stand loving both of your lives especially when the father wasn't a Willy keep rider of my Turlough with no floor to ceiling window in vision of virgin like in the old house but

I can get over that with a father gone and a father want which has supplies from the first for the last but I must be very careful which mates through love and can strive at the same time.

Do you think you control the heart of a jewel? Do they know what they are doing? Know, no. That is alright at what age in what eon?

They are paireynials, perennial flowers of a rock pathway from the garden to the do of the savanna hued as a jewel as old as the fossils that are the nail of wood the mortar of brick and stone. As I am to you is your play on "me" as am I the universe, through time because what else is ticking the heart?

There is a man sitting on a fulcrum at a desk dishing out cups of positive and negative ion water and you have a judge and you question His, if I go beyond the vanishing point in a puff of smoke do I trade or buy shares on the stock market? In the window of the garden know Rey no for you have produced the truth of a one eyed a metropolitan burg eyed man. This sail is set extremely of love this daily bread to purchase the jewel of Aladdin's lamp a new bed so that I can sea blue with both eyes again.. The only problem is that the I jewel is in the smoking cave. Lips that do not touch tobacco are the frontier. She must have his impulse of something dividing the night from the day, a coffee in or out, or a new bed and talk and medicine. Two eyes to see brilliantly and hips that softly reformed and kept are needed for the soul of the final frontier.

Your opinion isn't entitled if it is of the personality that by laughter you are stealing souls. "I try hard not to" said Rey. Reyna added a new bed John and I was temporarily blinded by the commotion and upset because I felt in advance somebody was tricking or treating me. Literature would mean a new roommate. The next day I washed my hands in porcelain water and they became sparkling clean.

"What are we Kong, Phlegm under the constitution?" asked Eric. A lass it isn't although King Kong with "me the universe" and the virgin it might be. I'll have to ask Eric of her when I ask.

So Eric left to do his morning thing and Rey again approached with his anti Loki mischievous soul, stealing and dealing hysteria which he calls the best medicine humor. His technique is to chiropractic as much as he can, circumstances providing from both the patient and environment, then to George Washington Carver the emotions all with the logic if his soul isn't stolen his can be hysterical and if yours is stolen you can be hysterical also.

The virgin soothes my one leg that I have left to stand on and waits. The time in the morning is up to her not hysteria and I second that motionless felt but invisible soothing rest despite what Rey thinks. Stilled and soothed and this ship not rocking too much, the hysteria fades into good laughter and my soul although weakened as in a sauna still hot but smaller broken heart than thought enjoys a good laugh in steady taught.

I could tell you more but why chance the growing to the speed of light analysis. In Nature all growth is a purposeful stretch or length involving months years. Why do you ask by what speed you grow with nature? Babies! To understand the distinction of the speed of light to a holy moon ringed by blood red clouds tonight. You see too far in a glass eyed paradise waiting and watching for the speed of light. It is my time on earth you ask for. When will the real heaven come to you in a cloudy moon opening? Are you appointed to the elect, to the entertainers, to the wise of science, to the wise of healers, to the wise of faith, to the door of life's business, to the deep blue see of the universe? When is there time to see God's growth of time which is gravity of planets and suns and spin and natural delights and distance election of wrong conclusions of fury from that which is a false light. When my space is my face of land has home marriage rights and those are rights and neighbors to love guarantee thereof.

Other than that you search in the speed of mirror light by day for natures growth. Why can't you search for the slow midday sun which is space and where the moon is a delight instead of the speed of light? Which personal appearance menu mirror slows to seek a beau, lemonade stirred in the shade? Seeks as well the nights of deep ringed moon verse, growth of eternal universe. Why do you mix the two as the day to grow rises? And ask which is blue and sky and which blue is depressing and mean. Which planet is brown or red or white and blue and which is full foliage green? Only to sup by milk for breakfast when you ask is it lunch off beans. And green is from the blind of blue. I rest all night as the wax grows in my ears. Sorrow is pain, rested up it isn't here. Time weights for know man and know man has found a woman here with the chase at no speed of strobe light, with a two candle bulb hungsunfood and mugs head of beer.

*W*ell deep enough that the sad does rise as medicine is given in the shades drawn late dawn. The medicine and rising charge nurse clearly sponged my mind clear from eight balls with tails of dark power fighting over my head at night while sleeping a comfortable naive innocence a lamb in a cool hall of care by medical staff. What is bad my nurse, and what is good, what is your opinion? Living as a drunk bar dodo with enough business that knowledge is leisure in senior age. Or without enough business but sincere about the knowledgeable the intelligentsia in ripe age of journeying that did enough to be kept by himself as a serious journeyman.

Seniors scratch their own backs. Dress in black attractive expire people who are slumbering then knight fame no matter what their life. My mind is woken up and bamboozled between the ghost of my mother haunting my soul I see her and it makes me feel off balance like a drunk drinking in an inn. A pattern of a gold tailed hawk barely visible appears in the morn-full hallway knowledge of the cutting edge with no business except to survive with beauty in nature. The hawk flew and I knew its pattern cleared as I worked out in the gym. Physical therapy wasn't from a mammal of weight a dog to trip up my legs walking but of a bird one on the telephone wire and one the faintest shadow of a hawkishness when flirting and sweating and exercising. Maybe you should call me John Hawk I don't know. I did know a Ron Hawk in school. My eye that doesn't know what switching medicine effects looks like is playing bingo several hours later with its head twisting to the right or left of reason of Eden,. The ghost is still with me suckling my mind and from a second elevation of hall luminous in my bedroom. The forest that I now see since a judgement day I can see separately from the trees.

BOGUS BASIN ISLAND

There is on a southern sea near where a coastal island shore rolls the north and south latitude into longitude of east and west the island of Bogus Basin. This is the name because they searched for gold and treasures here and to no luck in the hidden veil they found only beach sand, conglomerate cliffs and yes beautiful surf. The money was far away not in surplus in this year but because previous years hadn't been as lean as these of the war. Houses beautiful houses were partially built and left and to Wright with no income left only to write on from the far away surplus of good banking surplus days. This keeps the island with a rich a population as it had when first built.

The exception in the past being the wealthy moving loads of building material in and around the shore to build a few great houses. And the remainder, paisanos of faith and servitude to god and mankind.

Among this population are dogs cats and a man named the Catalan of Kobe, "it isn't all bad', or Bogie. Now let me explain. Please, around please please. Catalan is a superintendent of education, Kobe a prince on the hoops field, and they had plenty of energy and when mixed with an education makes a yearning for adventure far from the sickly bed but in an errant cross over the center line of a roadway confusing through the roof weigh. This energy and weigh and if you will pardon me way, an educationalist and an athlete after having one meeting reminded me of Einstein's famous equation at least fleetingly by the sunset light combed over surf all day since the morning light.

There is the theifs work that removed their nuclear power plant. This is "not all bad" as Bogus has handsome faces and prefers to surf and one of them is Bogies. But what is it to eat and sleep with a roof over your head provided by a rich man to a poorer, banditry?

Thessalonians 5: 2-4 "For you yourselves are fully aware the day of the Lord will come like a theif in the night. While people are saying, "There is peace and security," then sudden destruction will come upon them as labor pains come upon a pregnant woman, and they will not escape. But you are not in darkness, brothers, for that day to surprise you like a thief". The theif on the island of bogie is like the harpooner from Moby Dick but he appears as banditry of car, key and lock, and valuables that make your assets. The difference in this day and age is the island of pacific has woodies and is a mixture of rich new and Godly beliefs. The Boogie in this beach front island is a asset the harpooner can lance as it is a type and a line that the whalers want bogied into their ships locker. And malfunctioning poor car must have severe maintenance problems and be taken in for repair and service. A race eh Catalan? Different people from different islands of Tarzan co-inhabiting and inter mixing please please please include the beautiful girls and handsome faces of Bogie's for what do you think keeps the ownership of this vehicle a solitary ride? Riders of two three and even four. Moby Dick is after my car a bogey? Cupids lance fired from the whalers port bow. This and ownership of love which untangled is fair court no matter what age. Aye it can not hurt Catalano unless severely tangled and some of the bogie faces are not that and know how to manage money and they know the masters race and are properly in the lane and therefore circuit and do not know the whalers harpoon for they are fortunate and properly legal and legitimacy a priority of love. There are fortunate beauty and fortunate paisano living as neighbors and the race outside their doorway goes on and on from daybreak to midnight. Be One with the ocean and find several friends and feed them a 100$ and they will find the kitty to feed as the jew said leaving the sphinx before exodus and the whaler will turn to coast guard and the harpoon turn to a road race and only finding the One and the right roadway will make this more or much less than love a maintenance. I would also like to be a whaler turned to coast guard once a fortnight there. There are so many car types and makes competing for attention of sounding rights as a jet airport thousands of miles to the north in a place called Fresno.

This just could be lead left lead right and slosh bucket inn schwack over the falls to my feet sole and sitzen sie into the love handles of my chair legal and legitimate a priori fact. Take my hand Kitty and let it be. The real ether the real talk of safety. And spread your fingered hand into my hilarity as you know you should be the guardian of assets of when we should hide, when we should go out, and what is up at sea. Is it a sinker on a fishing pole? On this plateau where Moore camps and it is like a sleeping bag which comforts the morning dove as it is one of the most gentle and least richly over protected birds that is the beginning and the end "you can't take it with you" 1 Timothy 6:7 "For we brought nothing into the world, and we can take nothing out of it." The dove flies the gentlest of creatures on the plateau of sea and is a beginning morning of consciousness as the moisture hangs in your eyes from the trees and wipes the seepseas.

Wipe the sepses oil as you can smell the feathers as well as be terminal islanded boat and bait shoved into one another. The sinker is it hurts Moore when the beginning morning light turns into a morning doves coocoo, Kitty, that is smashed has not as much a chance as the rich birds whose hands are in the hilarity. And this verse from Timothy says riches are from the evil? Not always true for there are gentle and wise rich men who can hold the tinker belle in their palm.

There are rich wise gentlemen and ladies who can hold the morning dove so she doesn't sink. And they hold her once you have mentioned it as you dove are not to be dropped as a pentacle from the shoe aisle.

Goods for good people real industry goods can keep you up. Matthew 6:19-21 "Do not store up for yourselves treasures on earth, where moths and vermin destroy, and where thieves break in and steal. But store up for yourselves treasures in heaven, where moths and vermin do not destroy, and where thieves do not break in and steal. For where your treasure is, there your heart will be also." So it is said by Matthew and true. Peter found Jesus on the rooftops so we didn't sink. And yes he found his fishing again the fishing for the souls of man.

Each business has a roof or used to and each company a condo or section of real estate or business has a roof but the sink is for the plumbing and plumbers and their water gravity harness detectives of business. And that is rise o bread? Doing right is rise. It is where your heart is as in Matthew. Then watts this Newton a book that is write down my alley for my heart. Brothers say I wish you a Good life better than you had before. Keep it upper Brentwood says Moore. There, there are many good roofs that see faces of heaven and the Saint Nick of Christmas. It is the American dream. The alley has its own support a cubicle an ex-garage band and a lass but alack some detectives too.

So does a coffee shop and I should say cube because that is its shape. The bird goes up and with no shoes of riches by a priest tying her down looses that as simply as the prince of the morning dove could loose his head. The garage band cubicle can come down on you like a cube then I run to the coffee shop. That is without riches that aren't to be taken with you. But why Timothy we aren't nearly ready to be taken up yet. We are to love art on this world. She tries I try and down top and head blown away just feathers and a turn into the wind.

We are not made of cracked mud but this is the Salvador Dali-Disney film "Destino" portrayal with time being expended. So how else can I feel as shoved first by terminal island second by gone with the wind and third by goat pentacles and physiques of bird. The Rich Man and Lazarus, Luke 16:19-31 "There was a rich man who was dressed in purple and fine linen and lived in luxury every day. At his gate was laid a beggar named Lazarus, covered with sores and longing to eat what fell from the rich man's table. Even the dogs came and licked his sores."

"The time came when the beggar died and the angels carried him to Abraham's side. The rich man also died and was buried. In Hades, where he was in torment, he looked up and saw Abraham far away, with Lazarus by his side. So he called to him, "Father Abraham, have pity on me and send Lazarus to dip the tip of his finger in water and cool my tongue, because I am in agony in this fire." "But Abraham replied, "Son, remember that in your lifetime you received your good things, while Lazarus received bad things, but now he is comforted here and you are in agony. And besides all this, between us and you a great chasm has been set in place, so that those who want to go from here to you cannot, nor can ayone cross over from there to us." "He answered, "Then I beg you, father, send Lazarus to my family, for I have five brothers. Let him warn them, so that they will not also come to this place of torment." "Abraham replied, "They have Moses and the Prophet; let them listen to them." "No, father Abraham," he said "but if someone from the dead goes to them they will repent." "He said to him, "If they do not listen to Moses and the Prophets, they will not be convinced even if someone rises from the dead."" I walked by the edge of the small stairs which leads down to the beach. The cliffs before shared no abutment that could take the lateral as well as the vertical forces of the spirit as the stairs might. There is no cross planted on the cliff. The homeless I am not sure shared the off the rocker feeling of falling, going down like Judas where you have lost the edge in competition. This feeling is nullified by the surf on a good day at least when Jesus is coming back. Space the possible habitant which is from where they have fallen limited greatly by lack of funds is a place of peace and is sight. It gathers on a plateau more than the tides gather the waves at the beach and since the monarch of a technology in heat of a courtesan can be nightfall on the plateau with appearance engineering, physics engineering and to Dr. Eric hypnotherapy it is now genetic engineering.

The genes of engineering keep a cooler arm inside a cars window with the air conditioning on than their fathers genes that burned his arm skin in Hades until he asked one of his three sons if he could move to a cooler latitude. He said yes. The father removed his long sleeve shirt that covered his burning arm in the tropics and went alone without his wife she went into seclusion into a bachelors room. It is a plateau that needs an uphill climb. Since the space station floats, the uphill climb is to get there and break out of the gravity. The sun is my fathers courtesan and the earth is his monarch. I also on my own now find it an uphill race on which the suspension of my car does not work well on float except to see his shining face floating high on the ceiling fan. There is a down from maintenance and at the end of the night "all is well safely rest". The sun is still a burning courtesan and hot air goes up as cooled air goes down. Space is political and international and now a political and international park at the beach floating a loan from it's monarch the city and the sun still the courtesan. And one park next to the coffee shop but at the market you can still find the fruits food and nuts you want at the park the correct abutment of lunar and wind and sea in his office and manage them as a right brain cortex Dr.Eric. On my plateau and He by prayer and sight, easy on my eyes: rest my mind, her hands clasped together found my eye and myself by walking between the cars and looking over the sea. A rich girl, she found my eye in glasses and I found hers on the banister at the edge of the beach coming back to me through the cars the joined eyes of space-out or if you will "my space"; the houses at the edge of the beach an architectural dream. I have had a lack of dreams since they burned out on the sun the global warming effect only countered by "el Nino". This is the limit of my true space experience. The lasting time I had done this I had "my space" from a poor man at a retail area that has since been torn down by the city my eye from one of several coffee shops from the eye of AA homeless man. He was poor like Lazarus. Now my lasting time is expanding into women and I now come in heat. WOMAN a new dream of ages, time immemorial, and years of mother of invention, as a fellow swim team member would say in a competitive heat of racing and getting your tobacco and fire only quenched by mineral water at the end of the race. Where is the wonder of woman with myself in twos.

Where four art thou place my love as if Mother Nature tells a good place to navigate to or where you do an uphill climb out of the bachelors quarters so that there are hopes for two three and even four. That is the question. You are at the market the home of the Godly with quiet eyes of light. Is this Life Magazine published 40 years ago. You are again on the banister of the street loving the ////"no delete" as much as the quenching by mineral water. You are again with the prayer of continuance at the railings by the beach who when eyes meet I can relax and rest my eyes and therefore my mind. You are again with the birds and coffee that goes up and with know shoes of riches by a hero, by a baseball player, what it is written and said SSL to the hearts. This race had the end reins that gave relatives pneumonia more than burn especially in monsoon rains and latter dry heat. This is modern my love as you have tried to show me. You can tell a man by his fruits. MATTHEW7:15-20 "Beware of false prophets, who come to you in sheep's clothing, but inwardly they are ravenous wolves. You will know them by their fruits. Do men gather grapes from thorn bushes or figs from thistles? Even so, every good tree bears good fruit, but a bad tree bears bad fruit. A good tree cannot bear bad fruit, nor can a bad tree bear good fruit. Every tree that does not bear good fruit is cut down and thrown into the fire. Therefore by their fruits you will know them." Then I ask you what about the dress and the dressing. Some of you know my address and come to my window the Jehovah group. And today a Jehovah family with a daughter wearing unusual for the modern haughty a dress. Is this to dress my fathers arm or as genes are similar mine in case of fire? It is hot today and the address of the haughty only known by phone and some good ones SSL like you Jehovah. In this coo coo kitty morning doves pictured nest it is the sun and I only have goose bumps to cool and my skin draws taught with the thermodynamic reaction. Then you come to my window Jehovah family side locked not without a Shepard but a-lass? what is the shade of the sun to you my home, your homing to Shepard. To the retail of the surf and sunburn and it's industry. Better than Moses law a "what" mainly police the area O scout but let them come to the stake not.

That tastes of scallion pancakes to cool the tip of the tongue of the purple rich Lazarus and you are gifted now

in heaven by the family side locked was Novalis? I have
my problems they are greatly helped by family side locked
the abutments say however it is like you are going away
to school now, high damn time says my father. And that
answer is only the sun with only goose bumps to cool until
the template the computer room has the moist morning
awakening and another paper to write from a living great
man a professor of thought; blonde brunette or prostate
how are you going to get it out of me, earth water or fire,
check or bank card.John 4:1-40 The woman at the well.
"In his encounter with the woman at the well Jesus broke
three Jewish customs: first he spoke to a woman; second,
she was a Samaritan woman, a group the Jews traditionally
despised; and third, he asked her to get him a drink of
water, which would have made him ceremonially unclean
from using her cup or jar. This shocked the woman at the
well. Then Jesus told the woman he could give her "living
water" so that she would nevers thirst again. Jesus used the
words living water to refer to eternal life, the gift that would
satisfy her soul's desire only available through him." And
Kobe returned to Catalan he was a little more rested and
Catalan had explored the byways more. Kobe wanted to see
girls and his invited guest was Catalan. Likewise Catalan
let him stay as he was wiser to his ways. Kobe the hustler,
the beginning actor, the expensive poor down on his luck
of the monarch his eyes red, a wayfarer of the courtesan
with a need for a cool drink. One a guest of the other an
ace of jacks to be played for Kobe's queen, Catalano the
pretender king older and more wore torn and in need of

ladies in waiting. "Wait", this was the prayer answered to both as they went to the Mission and prayed. In between the thousand stars of night in new constellations a grace period if at night and peaceful because at morning comes the gathering light until sunset. And women come in heat Kobe? The RF from the law by night or you can find them by day asking "too much" for the perfection in finery clothing dressed or dressings not. A thermodynamic toughness to the skin needs the light to be courtesan and a home its monarch the richer the finer the dressings or not. As seeing is believing but then again O doctor so is the heart the lungs going gasp fresh air is life much more than nicotine or smoking I now know. Most of all the mind of the soul it is fooled by the masses in wifi satellite and phone but not by soul mind when experiments are extended and privately expanding. So Kobe what are your adorers blond brunette or prostate. The home knot inlaid being the monarchs earth rain and fire. The bank card or check obviously in reconstruction where the rf lights and ladies come. Food of Foo you righten me from a home that does not fall so easily.

Therein is also RF computer heat of ladies and lights. Where is what two for four do you telluride this expanding experience? I heard divorce was in the wind from desperate mothers and housewives. Ah sew only from the ears of "asking too much" of perfection of clothing of him dressed or undressing not as the mother walked down the street. A thousand stars has the evening sky and the mourning dove gathers at first electric light. This lasts only for 5 ot 10 minutes I Haight under Catalans release but not his skin the goosebumps of the sun.

You have an energy to be reality when where and if we both visit enough not longly but also not to quiet. In Quest I can't find these women I am not allowed but then again Quest has long been too quiet.

Let us go joyriding, Jehova only offers the beast for government anyway I say we offer it for moonshine and joyriding it is the pickup mode to my generation. On movie Riddel High School On. What is the reaction to an actor be he licked sores by dogs at a rich mans table or the son of the rich man himself. Kobe you look like an Egyptian and do you or only I see the seven pointed star?

REYNOLDS AND PLUMBING

Reynolds does the earth reign perfectly and do earthquakes calm the motion even where they do not have fault zones? Ah Jawan diet the bloats and what rain forest is this you call with no mountain structure? Reynolds is Ben Lawrence and his eternal infinite vision il a coma who was a doctor was that God without a lord in spirit in the sky of adoption as I saw sleepwalking A lord of body earth power and the highest not he? Is it all in the mind like a doctor of the mind diagnoses? Prognosticate to me Rey. Ah Jawan doctors get their medicines from plants and animals and the earth LIKE we all eat in our stomach but our sol comes from the liver the heart the brain the highest say the Greeks. Today I am not eating I because I have a doctors appointment tomorrow, I ate plenty yesterday. Which eye do you have to sea? There will be an answer from the people and a crying out murmur the bird the plant the man the fish and what food? It is a matter of days weeks months years as the lord knows them and what is time to he when the virgin girl appears to me from answer from email note from India in he hours. Is your soul from days every day is a new day unto weeks months years or do you think your soul is made of email. Man does not eat by email alone but in this case by an okay for medicine which brings every day is a new day and with a thump and lump a new year and with that a new stream and fish jumping and a beginning thought. Then there is food for thought but remember the supply line and who saves your mortal life so it could have a born again soul the second days of your life even after he's father and mother have perished. This is a little bitter pill like the willow did not bend in time to save the fig. They were not born of the willow food for thought email yet deep in the Lore they were with you in the dreams of transfigure de of the virgin girl from India by email. So is the food that is the food that is in the thought because it also is from y ancestors paid dues. So is the email because there is an eternal infinite which grows and develops and even likes tinker bell in this day of days and there was a tinker bell Lord knows in the past that could not email a virgin to appear but did have a house {full of adaptive and adoptive eyes at see. You sea Rey as it is a great everlasting power of earth the light dancing on its wave tops the sea in a freshness of rain the oath of the home the house of lord but what is the similarity to the Himalayas the food chain email girl from India for that was the freshness too in the medicine the food for thought. No man lives by email alone. You sea in a ship in the Himalayas gay ism by a dream marked Claremont maintenance. This makes days of every days wears and weeks and the food starts at day one and months and years It has also been in the mountains of the tinker bell. The ship of Sini not in the Himalayas ga: ism birth of the pre reborn was with the infinite but not at day one of the eternal the sea. Th ship of Sini of first family was born to the Lord in Unitarian sheet lighting rain and thunder and latter day on a frosty afternoon hail high in the Gabriel mountains a sister city of Greece- you know. Doth you spiel from the hail speak from the thunder and and have knowledge o mystical poetic philosophy from the Lightning from Gabriella a sister mountain nook named wilderness park in a toga? Fosters frosty Frost the poet as he calls him by phone lack of email knowledge then don't you know has written what? A book of transcendental poetry.

much akin to the swami's or Solana. That book talked like but a weak adversative particle, generally placed second in its clause, This book talks of eternal sea Socratic still but with styling hell pressing war and thrones and the togas are long gone replaced by the light of the hair and those burning bald and the next generation jet and turbo search engine. What is in my gene I think is keeping an understanding of the new O almighty sock pressed like time wine into something to comfort my pains my pains of the war of garden mine or garden yours. No war is a rose garden while it is fought. It strains the impossible to find the new that in not alone is to be food for machine nourished understood and remembered. Man does not live by email alone in a minor plastic air dam. I have lost the jaw mask of iron by the love of the virgin last night but she has filled in my heart with night softness. The virgin I see in my room Ah Jawan but it is a neighbor the girl in the zipper of my thyrsus that has me coming to quiet the see with soft nylon. I am thrones in the liver when she does this because you Sini I am at three places within minutes apart at the same place burning hair out until I can't see any ether any more.their friends arrive and take the cup of wroth the sun with no substance of even ether of zipper or burning hair out and give that back to me the zipper of some money re-thrones at both or three places. Reynolds you are the zipper of Moore's thyrsus the quiet at see. And do you know what you will find when your virgin comes? A wrinkle on your leg as the Wozniaks used to say in the banana belt of the Sawtooth or an iggle if you are keen to philosophy that has to if I let you be calculated when the virgin comes so the fire department knows where you are and can navigate by search logic. Friendly but no calabash these androids and what of the virgin is she a pipe dream vision or something more real? Ah Jawan what is real is in the seat of your pants in this Baxter Moore forest. Baxter flew do you and where to? Seat of the pants you say Reyn?

There is nothing to the seat of the pants but a toadstool but the legs Reyn is where the power is even more so the sight of your eyes and the brain and back which calculate. So I hop to it moping around the room before the vision comes clear I am a little bit brought up in Sini. And this vision of a virgin spreads for a mile between two or three places. To escape the androids a miss is as good as a mile. When banking this vision into a logo for money the androids understand also. Wrap on Reyn am I merely an old age with poor toadstool to the bank or do I have heart to be softened and ironman left as younger than spring time when the flowers blossom. Ah Jawan KEEP IT and most men or "'! omen in their youth or prime can make 10,00 sun gazing can you? Calculated squares pieces or nerds of the wiggle Rey? 'Schroeder' "hides his emotions behind the mask of the fool, but he often shows his wounded heart." A thought to be nourished, Am I brought up by texting then ear rings as the rainbow idea jumps with afrikaners acting to modulate the security whine across the fountains and pool at UCI. Ore with the establishment and eating more at the commons to nourish the thought? Schroeder you see I need a radioactive disposal_battery to power my kitchen's so that I may eat and this is what I call the homeless in a state of drunkenness. Sitting Before Christmas children show them their true skill. There is no blueprint Before Christmas but afterwards I SISi. I have an I. I have an ego. And I must abandon the sound of everything ness for that is I without music. For wh~t is I with the social media if I am to accept the children of After Christmas? I and ego may put aside the space between two doors dim in the light like cats eyes maybe like the mocking birds nest and by day mockingly move like a motion a game even professed as a physique of space. Two doors too me as the before and after Christmas Children or even three places is my I and ego in quietness of the first door in social media of the second door for I will or will not drop the third place for the After Christmas Children will I? I must put two doors asleep like the computer to sleep and in the new next day by morning light must pull myself from the shades shadow just at dawn when I awake. I Will be new and I must have life separate the sepses from my eyes in the light for it is only time old man time lacking the infinite light of the After Christmas Children's previous knowledge through the key hole of doors. Love me Schroeder softly murmurs the next door neighbor virgin's friend and although she is in her house and the house of Sini she makes love among friends and this girl of the rising sun the morning star has love for me and as the blond eye of mine has already died it is a sepses that also.

She comes in my new and changed diaphragm heart at first I know my died eye then there is life in my belly and diaphragm as she makes old man time street walk by attaching to a piece of my modem. Ah the sidewalk and herself and the car and then she drives away and rushes and with no money from me gives me a shaky less arm a diaphragm newness aimed perfectly. And I am sun rising in the house of Sini seeing with the sparrows and mocking birds singing although they not in a rush like this lass was and now must step to the sidewalk and go close to the sea for the new guts have lived to go back to the sea again. I bloats don't know what the virgin is doing because bloats I don't the virgin. Is she swinging in the trees for her Tarzan? I, eye must be careful for they setting android traps like the cherub at the edge of the see garden on the way to sea eats this morning. Schroeder this is Rey. The disposable radioactive battery a drunken homeless says there is a 7.4 earthquake in the Himalayas in Nepal. Is this going to unfounded the bloats which is what all they are worth anyway. My machine got abecause bloats little unfounded and tipped over from none thing I could see hear or find who did this I needed a new brake handle. From none thing I could or find or hear beau· straight from my eye came the vision of the virgin. All this in my lap from the atmospheric river which extends separates retracts extends and separates again as in a dance that isn't dizzy? Schroeder says "cat fur dog fur pants of Ralph trash what is this a straight jacket?"

The straights of Gibraltar the atmospheric river of So. Cal the earthquake of Nepal in So. Cal a Shakespeare witch? Ah lord there are as strange things in these times of war stranger than fictions. Schroeder continues that is if I can include a message to him. At 1:69 am at night. There are none things and some things and their order this is how the computer works. At 2:85 am the pipe dream murmurs there are willows that don't bare fig there are maidens tied to the mast that have nothing to front and press against. the wind but a thumbnail sketch and now we are at 1 :95am. Are the ripeness of your fruit telling One what is to bare through time uncharted pressing Over the Queens none things as as in null and void? Jehovah Witness says. You can tell a man by his fruits. Are these some things?

Suppose a woman has no breasts and a man has no children are these none things? Is uncharted time swinging through the winds of none things and some things? Is time uncharted and variable no says the clock and calendar that is how we schedule. Suppose c the sleepy time the happy pill does make time seem charted to thoughts half coming from the days conscious a~d half C?oming from the the days semi conscious night time variable with the soul in different moods. In which_does the fish jump better for a beginning thought' There is no night fishing when do the sands pull the grunion? There is. There is no day fishing when does the trout jump for Mosquitos? There is. So the fish jump· better for a beginning thought by day and night so they like to find their foundations for food or forever. then. Do you really have a feeling for the conscious or semi conscious? None things and some things from the iggle and fish and foundations for food or forever. Can this be a foundation of the world and does man not eat by email alone? This is the virgin's vision. What if the foundation of the world in my feet wrapped is in the virgins booties but then again supporting by what power in my legs to left Schroeder from heavy heavy hangs over thy head children's games played on wooden door jams and hummingbird bird trees earth to two places too many and all that is near and in a short circuit. These are foundations of two halves of the brain working the adolescent neurotransmitter so that one arm plus one arm with the feeling knowing in eternal this being the circuit of one arm plus one arm the other arm and what do I have Vishnu and the foundation of Hindu at the door of old Jehovah. Which came first the egg of the hummingbird or the hummingbird for fly fly fly away we must. Where from thou zipper flies and planes of the Topic Colorado River universe thyrsus Schroeder is this real time ground or merely here there everywhere or 2X2 Dixie music time. There is a water hose for many farms as the world has better or worse and that the meek shall inherit - yes but why am I to look down at the earth while you look up and then reverse. Places everybody of four arms instead of positions of silk although you have that also. The atmospheric River of So. Cal flows silk and knows position and although the silk flows like rain the positions do not touch for the richer or poorer unless we camp and then only in a lodge. Is this freedom of religion from mankind of music or mankind of photography as the hummingbird hovers zooms and dives as we were in New York? Is this the place at my feet of Vishnu the cars sure sound like it dam tempo. Crap Kirk I just did or is this real? Four arms has God is what Vishnu is. Moses is walking along the hump route where the Christians have to flee or be as strong headed as the nephelometer. And I have to bank this mess Noah some where in China or the sun doesn't rise again. Is this sunshine long and cool and irrelevant except for money. Money is to be made and Kirk Vishnu Christians Moses Noah China and the Nephelometer know this. For the email is not free even though it was described as freedom. Even the bread is not free. And this Freedom of money is so a quirk to me. Avast thee lubbers and if we have sun then we have power and warp 10 off the planet into the solar system we QO and later what Kirk the universe. Fly fly fly. hummingbird zipper flies or jet since the sun is banked we have power. D!d confusions say something about fusion as JD Power was honoring? When you are in the lame duck with feet of Vishnu step away from the local high pressure zone of a changing corporation or zot you too could have a stroke and that would nullify everything you could learn about sex at the age of Abraham. I asked the man in the sky do Buddhists Christians and Hindus feel like the same earth is under their feet when they are lame duck and walking with the whale. Rather than the sea for this minute is it the roots of trees the feelings in the soul of your feet? And that for some includes surfing and waves the foundation of the world? I am in Dana Point. the home of Hobie and Corky Carrol. Wave and particle physics 'and gravity and lame duck and foundations of the world. Do you really have a feeling for them in the conscious or semi conscious world? Is this a daydream at Starbucks where the climate is rain and sea or Mediterranean? I did a slide Clyde of chairs Clyde is what we used to call the camel, from nothing ness to aware ness. Is this awareness of writing not stupidity? It's. the young girl being introduced to me by her father first setting I think in a fabulously wealthy family so the plastic clothing of her thyrsus can flow to me through windows by her fathers steadfast and kind attention to friendship on bending knee.? Is this the awareness of writing not stupidly? That is one way wealthy families are made.w c. Schopenhauer said once comparing one of his thoughts to Nietzsche that what is important is the WILL or that which holds from within. This is holding the soul mind and liver to the body as it is thrown "up against the wall" as the demonstrators of Vietnam Nam remarked? Know. If one is racing in tight shoelaces and motocross suit can end living in that body even after the virgin saved your mortal life is it that it could be said that this is her power of God too for virgins are to be seen and what touched? Touched says bonjour is crazy, and is it the power of the virgin, the virgin and her city, or the power of the eye so that they can be seen in public, so· I and ego receive the cities round and end up very off balance and against the wall in my room. This is one mile away.My life is saved therefore save able after the motocross suit gets put on or as one could imagine the Vishnu of four arms, the straight jacket, seemingly balances even the bloats and normal thyrsus on tip toes in semi gravity and are not

8 ~ A car higher than a kite Schroeder makes an thrown off balance but yes thrown. -:_.:: onto the fwy run from Sini checked out by a pro and finds what's this connections?zippers? A sort Rey from car to God knows which car here there everywhere seemingly in a short circuit fwy distance. The short circuit high on baby shoelaces.which I brought the virgins medicine food and a vape must be seated in the drivers seat checked out by a pro so that the brain expanding doesn't get tangled carrots connections zippers. In a distance one can see the right car in the right place at the right time connections that later with a pro driver can put the reality gravity of a drivers seat under lanes with a vision dot state patrol null not there. In the drivers seat a reassuring foundation of the world

gravity feels past and present and a cities round feeling past, lean again feel the steering wheel and drivers seat from hungsunfoo semi gravity feel to hungsunfoo Gravity feel. Round the pier round on the ramp hungsunfoo, have. YOU ever seen semi retired Abraham in his race? \- il

"':? I have and at dinner the plastic baby shoelaces are released to another dinner over beer wine and tilapia. The refrigerator is the server ~ it feeds the fat in the other rooms of a four units. One to five passengers in a car? John Emery Morse may 2015 It is the gurgle it feeds "the morning coffee" an intestinal system that talks to a lonely man. A son of God that makes me think of life by morning gurgle feeding his bread to the masses I? In my room. Yes a doctor streets of the doors blocks away just I and my refrigerator and computer and several chairs and bed to climb out of and Me what the world is outside of I i in this case lets MAKE IT from beginning art to modem feeding systems. And what about the cars shall we have a wifi modem Feeding system or "air conditioning"? And Me for my room? Lets MAKE IT a wifi modem feeding system or "cooling food"? a ~ ? The purpose of the gurgle or bread is to hold with time being this in my room I know, so what Rey if ·Go is on the other beach or the other side of the mountain at the moment. He will be back. Holding that which is from within and having it alive and gurgle. Keep the notion that there i space between traffic clumps of throne warrior battleships and the quieter less horsepower more smooth although. more spring leaf traffic. Is the modem feeding system going to be making the long and smooth. It is made by you doctor you let me know. When we go the sun is at high noon but my room still sinks so Me and I travel "outside says the son of man." I just had French toast with coconut syrup outside and the son of man passed me by as Johnny is a nut a day husked by the gray hairs unto somebody of softly covered seat. -=-~~ ~ And after breakfast what then Johnny? AH a pipeful of tobacco and then cleaning out the beta particules the gold crown before nights brushing. It is Sunday after all and Jesus said some people may go and eat their corn while some may pray and the priests got as furious at them as the eventual fathers of thanksgiving got furious at the colonists. They demanded their only crown Son England to be out of their constitution wrongly or rightly. England had given them the first Magna Carta therefore written were the words of accord and broken those the words of the devil. This what the constitution of America did from Thomas. With stature of the thyrsus as strong, willing. dependable, magnificently practical, with genius aundant. What man said cat fur dog fur Ralphs trash and straight jacket made hell and heaven was a gold chalice for wine and a lance. And what man said the colonists pare with a sword and a gun? George. Thomas? There is transcendent and more as any Greek Roman civilization and was an exception. Abraham with the Indian princess who said to save captain John. $v,'$.-: ?.i And there was a doctor and he said to separate the words of the devil from the.words of accord by no man eats by email alone in • virtual reality. Was this man concerned with mapping out the country of Denmark like

Schroeder from Goethe or was he more interested in a doctor of the mind, like Shakespeare with one of the queens. This doctor could be above you or below you in superiority while feeding unconfused thoughts as a country window saw I through the looking glass is a country like Denmark a city like London and doctor like Switzerland that all migrated to America in communication to study as I LEARN THEREFORE I EAT BY THE SWITCH IN THE BRAIN. THERE IS A SWITCH THAT KEEP AN UNDERSTANDING OF THE NEW. ~ 0 Schroeder what is the brain the organ of mirror of manifest destiny of the universe. A mirror of the ears hearing speed of Newton as tangled by the speed of sound of Yeager. Have you ever seen Christopher Fuchs and Wired and a true little maiden of India growing into adulthood beside the wonders of India like a fire that has been burning for a hundred years and well could be the fire of mocking jay from IBM Sparks and his following the orders do it and hurry get a new bank debit ID and transparency on joint account. Lord to smoke in Baxter Moores forest you need a hole in the head and what is this the blinded neighbor was hurt in your head or bathroom as finite insanity screamed through your brain? She has gone to great lengths to not break your heart as the maiden was hurt and crying for help. Aye you have helped before Schroeder calling the police on a stalker and she this time called the police on the Wii that has hurt her. That which holds from within from two different entities people and places or one Schroeder. She has called and the entities are tangled from three or four places and hurt all the more because there is no responsibility to you to care Schroeder says Moses. And like the real Moses all you care with responsibility is to write on your tablet and snobbishly concerns IT. Aye Moses my snobbishly concerns are just what? The Schopenhauer Will of two apts. to help when my motor neuron disease can barely walk and the transparency of the accounts is a very meager number like old age or very young age nothing in the prime what she knows. 1_ q ':..:- Aye Moses you have a point though enrapt in your laws you cry although what consideration do I have as my cry is the house of Jude BC with the orders to hold for King David of Isreal and his return. Silent though she be this house eyes attracted to likewise the sound of silence of peace in the road she be a knowing entity exception of war and peace. And in my snobbishly wait just to use her time implores rape as if the lair was not seduced. My mea culpa better be good and for this I will turn to the lord that has wisdom at night as the Mormons have preached to me years before · and just several days ago. I had a dream which is as legal as Martins birthday in America. And the dream was bad as bad as her heart turned by a younger primes foolishness into sex of fire a song which when produced by the young prime they have in afterlife their kingdom the defense of which is left up to that genre era generation and dancing in position of riddance. Even though her positions in a car are as legal as the carnal positions in my car. This her generation understands. Entering through the keyhole of plumbing perception is a

Mystery which in several minds is all a heretic understands also so is the dream it is a mystery. My dream a mystery was that I was taken to a hospital and had the sensitive skin. on my penis surgically removed. Baptized by the Mormons maybe I was O Moroni there is still a man just a man that studied dreams and. their effect differing personality and what his name mighty women of two halves of the brain working or not Carl Jung? ~ ;..; ~ VI/ell as if I need a hole in my head from smoking so do I from that I Hold The Guilt. There is philosophy as well as deficient medicine mixed up to the high Lord. Alan Watts I remember if that is not as deficient as a nightmare mentioned that being without music is a prickly feeling LIKE a hedge hog. There is mentionable the short Henry story on Vimeo. Henry is a young hedge hog h~king a birthday and was born as prickly as a porcupine. He lives in a little hollow under the ground in a nice home. Henry bakes for himself a birthday cake and sits down to eat. Let them eat cake says the queen? We get a feeling Henry wants hugs. Not alone was the answer. So Henry invites friends. These arrive in the shape of balloon dogs that float and fly around his room. One he tries to hug but the balloon pops because of his prickly skin. Even a prickly hedge hog does not want to eat on the miracle of his birthday alone on this cake occasion. Some balloon dogs are friends and will be invited and some although looking in mirror looking glass very similar aren't friends and shouldn't be invited. How do you tell Henry which balloon dogs are going to pop because of your prickly skin and which aren't. If it isn't by looks and attraction love then the answer is to go to school with them for a year AND stay at your own grade level by era not appointed age of mind. I told you in law of insurance it was only for notations of ephemeral friendship collared from relationship into chatter of the legitimate and moral rnalority. w~l What determines guilt to the legitimate and moral majority?

Is it in context of man does not eat by e-mail alone thereby do not bite the hand that feeds you? Does your hand feed you fire as you eat. This approach war is hell to eat. In games it is the throne of fire and paranoia of the court I Hold The Guilt and the Hand if feeding feeding hell fire to anything but the enemy may be put in chains. So that is why the new logo from the enemies court's droids is you are under arrest as if they ever sang to Taylor swift in good virgins song. The hand that bit me this morning bit because it was eggs and ham and filled with fire the only substance in hell or war mentionable my supreme mistake. I do toke on a pipe don't you know but not the eternal fires of of the bad virgin's almighty eye state which the throne in all diabolical grandiose megalomania considers policy most righteously politics a unbalance of see sea SiSi justice under the hedge hogs beaming heavy heavy hangs over thy head. What is the problem supreme fire you have not counted on in the wiggle of squares and pieces that the prisons in your mind of slosh buckets could not put out. No fact of knowledge of what are you really are talking about makes money is why Kirk AND do not think that the hobby horse heals matter it takes the almighty buck to put food in your hand and genetically warped eternally non healing teeth to bite. My teeth your throne and kingdom. Do not bite the hand that feeds you it is fire. e ~ ~ It is not only determining the legitimate and moral majority ~ and sometimes these are in cohesiveness as a city and I think that is the only breadth I can speak of say Irvine but sometimes they are not. Like were we envisioned by almighty infinite and eternal design and this can't be proven as a scientific fact so we must believe and be taught survival of the fittest. Beautiful is this cities design, courts sports gym cosmetic walking all designed as if a lieu of boat atop land that has been known to be earthquake. SO beauty it is. And the survival of this beauty is what it is real estate. That's when survival of the fittest present an ecology of real estate where the best and brightest love in Irvine to learn. This makes evolutionary process that is keenly spirited if not driving too fast that is forward or progressive. What about the wreck and when you are driving too fast that does happen. Slacken me paradise Lord and place this on grounds of earthquake ecology yes sloppy slosh bucket real estate. The beauty of this design it goes forward at the same time it can go backward but only a minimal structure distance like the buildings feel in most... earthquakes but time is on the courts side anyhow long this goes on in falls the judgement but above ground in homeless wreck without locks instead of the abyss and time is determined this way as a hornelessness.vx sr Now after a short sleep on the front porch have one more thing to say about the legitimate and moral majority and this time I mean Eben Lawrence the neurosurgeon. Suppose in his coma and likewise I in my short sleep saw the beautiful eternal and there are as many definitions of this as there are philosophers, cried to come back to reality as much as Jesus Christ would cry out to his father when the worldly scheme of things would not allow the heavenly and this word means those below the eternal, rights to come to pass. Now Eben and I are mortals or are we of the heavenly and eternal too.:He cried when he recognized his son while comatose and heard the voices say he would have to leave this beautiful comatose and fight his way back to consciousness but he thought he could do it because of his son. Is this truly leaving the garden of Eden.

And I cried when I awoke from my nap and had to leave a beautiful waking of night or female infinite. Both of us have roots in the eternal and cried when we left that from the heavenly or infinite for the earth and he for family and I for the neighborhood. Is this loving your neighbor as you would yourself and the garden of Eden? So in the Baxter Moore forest the legitimate are the garden of Eden and the moral majority are those that love their neighbor as they love themselves. It is to be another every day starts semi conscious from the heavenly dream, rarely but sometimes from the eternal dream is A SONS day the speed of time. And what has the SONS day done wrong spoken about the garden and neighbors when it was the savior with the woman at the well that we were talking about. And who knows what 1. and ego knows Reynolds a Sons day a speed of time or the Savior Himself or. you Hamlet the king an ego supreme. I admit as Schroeder to Moses but when the Son is a policy a righteousness of politics judge and you shall be judged. This sadly to say is what the savior so legitimate didn't rule once upon high priests of sinners as a moral majority.:.:..~ <;? One does not know how plain it is until he has what he is not made of anymore. The pressure not, to be able to tie your shoes eh bloats? Testosterone boosters? Is this semi competition Abraham of a race or is this Moses loosing your Ten Commandments legitimate case and for how long in the fire of the desert moves until a life layer approaches and she stands on your right side and you sit at Debbie's the Mary right side and where in the doctors office. This is the throne being returned and is that where the moral majority lay a life· layer of high priests everybody is a sinner Moses I heard laid him low. So off with the medicine for three days until the side effects are understood. It is time simple time that has made him what he is not made of, any more and the throne for Claudius recounts Nero not his first born. Aye Aye Johnny has a rush rash but his eyes have become unblinded and exchanges bloaties no. Off with the medicine for a time yes unless it is the doctors order off with the bloats and the rash shall wait and sit an appointed time and find their Queen and her daughter and know it is only time old man time or is it you? Only time will tell and he makes us cars computers and yes Schroeder even rooms. Hawkeyes has met the eyes of the chain don't '...... let me pull yours once upon a time don't you know. This is a fairy tale?,..Even you Schroeder played with chain mail when you were a boy. ~ 0.. Same old same old. How do you have a soul that prospers as Henry a six inch hedge hog in virtual reality when you are really out o oculus studio? Rey show me the way show me the pathway is it testosterone boosters. Moses says I am not sure. I know so I think, I don't think, don't you know? You gave me eth answer when you were young and it was ridiculous and you had plenty then do you need ~ore now? I am just mad about saffron you're just mad about two fly. Do you know how a police puts in a light bulb? He has ten people hold the step ladder lift it up and turn it around. How is that answer one maiden is Spanish and one maiden is polish I drink to the queens and kings and Ben the rat the anarchist it is in design is the odd coupling or the odi couple. How does the soul..and it's temple prospect by polish odd coupling design or pre western anthropology, the study of the pyramid scheme? Know planned partnership of California puts the disciple at the mountain in Shasta County with a Spanish or Russian language okay. Both fault the USA already_though. That is the answer know no know. By doctors is the answer you gave me before if not by God alone but God includes many thing· if not everything all at once and the savior knew all children were in God's kingdom and to save your soul and wanted you to be prosperous and said you would do as many things as He and more.~ As the flowers for her love behold my labor and set to my niche my clothe: basket to the throne in the lieu I have received good tidings from the postal department which runs a box by Rita's Pennsylvania ice custard which young maidens can find and loose a love from their heart appearance and received my trader ice's food lot and in splattered drove there and picked up milk. The tower of the city had lowered first beckoning all well and goodness from this empire. Now I have drunken the milk a half a quart and going my way to the tea shop continue until at home and as I say what I see and see what I say the lithium crystals of the Lords and Mary's love sink into my right ankle with a string chain or wrinkle. This is medicine make love not war and I take that also usually mediocrely but on bright days of phosphates and furosemide see the net taken from my eyes so the son is made in the shades you are so bright.~ ::: ~ What is this my Lord a mea culpa I ha: not counted on that I say what I see and I see what I say is an airplane? Shall I not fly to England like I didn't know the airport was run by an English FBO and I didn't. Drive down the road of miserere of a Mormon O Lord be guise then and them as something from the Sistine Chapel. Clearly in the light I saw the Mormon Temple and that light shone as clearly as Philadelphia freedom be guise my headlights knew from from England, the Sistine, the Mormon I knew not where. This is until my lights went out and in eves arms fell asleep her.

Adam drive and asleep by your command..I woke late and you had taken me from Philadelphia's arms but had given me Mexican from windows of a tea shop a rich mom and teen I say what I see and them likewise scatter to the Sistine outside for besides my word my looks are not for duty of an emperors thyrsus. Mexicans are more interested in me than Philadelphia as can be testified by Lily wanting to know if I had a girlfriend and would like one. I need one is what she thinks..g, He made new knowledge as the son of God. Can you see the hierarchy Lord in the planet from space pictures? Do you get turned on to seeing the the Hubble scope pictures far out into space and wondering about the hierarchy that make the beginning and I won't say end because there isn't one we know of unless we calculate the billions per or of years. Yes. The belief in a hierarchy that is kind careful cheerful conscientious caring like God and he is to man and the fulfillment of the prophets like the sayings of Jesus as he brought His thoughts down to his disciples and kingdoms to be won. Thoughts of layers like life layers from the eternal to the heavenly this hierarchy to preserve time, life, I think of this and I think of John on Patmos and I think of the doctor of the mind and Shakespeare and is my life and all its layers I am of the nature seeing the heavenly believing in the eternal and in peace I have the support to compose what I see in the window of perception mediocrely a motor neuron gymnast of the eternal.

LAMENTS CHRONOLOGY

The stork was a raven. A mirror is a double airplane to me. A drunk on the road is being in two places at once. Suppose the perception of the world is defined by your culture nation and the cosmos as you look up and see the nation and its cosmos from where ever you are and is double? Suppose the time itself in a dream can reverse from real time and intuitively that warps the reality of time so I think and say it "doubles" time. There are two times one real that is forward and one reversed in one dream in particular. In this dream I was walking through a high door dark stained well appointed building a hotel so speaking of computer cubicles. Next I remember I was above the clouds where everything was white with a coast guard boat anchored there and some beautiful girls sunning. I was told to head down to land and in a space seat I descended and very unfortunately landed in Viet Nam in a putrid prison camp. The point is about time. The Emery laments are written from the Viet Nam prison camp which in the dream is after the computer hotel and the easter is in the clouds with the Coast Guard. The easter I wrote (small fonts) came in real time after the prison camp thoughts (large font), in dream time easter came before. I think therefore I can: from plurality lives and spirits can be tough on your heart. These are Emery's laments.

It is a toiling more than tooling world at fail time. From philosophy of authors in comparison to sway advantage of contracting do you sway the lumbar that is cut from time I will exist on this planet in comparison to the existential time of the house that you have built. The rites of the woman is her baby to choose the man she lives with the author with the cut lumbar or the contractor with the cut lumber is why I cry momma. They are both my brothers and sisters. Why did you cry grandma?

Somewhat likewise in shades of grey does pneumonia and blind spot spotty mean mathematics of arithmetic, medicine, calculus or gravity? The idea is there is a blind spot that keeps the unknown altitude oscillating drop of water above ones eyes or keeps the minds eye from recognizing the drop that falls from your mouth to your chin. Eh momma. The blind spot is where ones mind's eye doesn't recognize the where or what or what distance or what speed something say a drop of water or food particle is in front of your face. Likewise momma. There could be an aura around your body and seeing this may be blinded in the blind spot also. This aura is basically what I mean when I talk about seeing grey zones. Eh papa. Some grey zones are like aura protrusions which are greatly enlarged in size seeing a refrlgerator size in the kitchen or even a block away haze on the street. Eh grandma. The feeling of identity of oneself personality can vary as the aura is perceived as oneself greatly distorting the personality enlarging the space one feels he occupies and has the rights to occupy. Eh moma. The purpose of the eye as I see it is to define the space outline of ones body as he really takes up space and not an extended space body reality. Eh papa. The trick is to have the loo blinded partial sighting aura spot not be confused with the blind spot and at the same time have the eye outline the reality space of the body with gravity not dependent on aura or double light sources but to keep the charisma of the individual. Eh papa.

Papa, momma, grandma you have all passed now and all I have is my brothers sisters and cousins and yet your passing has stopped my heart as if It is my sin when some say it is genealogically the passing time and time is therefore yours and god has always risen. What about my soul? Is it in god's hands my pen, your house without seeing the entirety of the world and by the word to observe and write about a moarverse besides because genealogically a house is a Fowler. Without the pearls of the chicken house there would be no windmills. Unless you bump into her at rite-aid. Then why Tanyee does a feeling woman have know soul. If that's what you say then who created the wind huh we go Om by.

God a carpenter a writer. I have lost the head and hand in of papa then believing in him time replaced. He was a sun god a moon god a life saver kind of last meal that kept the morning time light of Egypt on the back of my head. A carpenter needs a hand to totally build a house a writer needs an eye to brush the pop teeth, the keen so that his hand be clean when he picks up a pen.

The company, they need a reason to be their own men and they need a reason to keep them from being their own men. Go for the pearls of the chicken man and you have reason against reason. Has it mellowed your spirit to sit still for a house? Is there a place beside someone in a home you wish to be mobilized to see. You miss the affluent the good life? What government is to afford prosperity and yet penalize the spirit of freedom? Time will for you have not understood the wins or loses over time. Police yourselves Boy Scout nature man that is that spirits right. Laissez Faire is the abstention of government interfering itself in the trade between countries.

May the mirrors of your mind be the seeing of double airplanes in the sky and clouds and be the abstentions of your time as it is mine until released not angry enough to be a sin by the oils of the pearls of the chicken of the windmills as the flour your mind.

Under dissent the reason to be men and the reason to not be men is the devils reaction against the son of god. I was once advised to play the devils advocate as a freshman and ended up or down or someways in a nuclear reactor in an out of body dream. All I knew was there are actors and reactors in your city papa until there was "moving time" of this earth and not just my mind. I moved once to Idaho for two years you papa and momma moved from Long Beach to Mission Viejo for fifteen years. Two years made fifteen. Trade time of the flu is a bell curve of two months not expoetrynential of pi are squared or is the circumference of the column ex's poetry? As eternal as 3.1415.... Why don't you try U and calculus of oscillating light of a ghost jet wind unheated of mirage of love may account owe lmao and use calculus and calculator rites at the drive thru: swimming. Different if there is no crisis why know crisis, but that started with they needed know reason and they needed no know reason. Dissent is the reason courier is that reasonable? Chad Matthew where are you? In the jungle tackle with the elephant ear botanists. And where did Brian go is he not eating his soup? He's having a smoke he will eat after Chad leaves and Matthew comes to the dinner table.. And what is that fly doing in my soup. I think the backstroke sir. Flies go to money like bees go to honey. When Peter's wing is broken how do you put his fly forward like Jesus? The worm s'ing and v'ing is diving into it's hole is the raven as it flies and eats and is at the mockingbird and satan holds your legs and damages them so you can't walk well and says Roger for your neighbor's raven beauty sake use the gait as your front door use Pantene on your shower, break a leg, and He breaks one and the ravens are egg eaters for him. Thus as I grow do I eat eggs or cereal with bananas milk with Oates and half and half my coffee? We are at different places in numbers, therefore time. The mockingbird dives as the raven crows hawk twice.

And I have been given life by picking the special K fruit of my neighbor eating the cereal for breakfast and receiving streaming FM and it and the life in my car. The secret Johnny is have plenty of protein drink first. It sprinkles then suns then rains then warms and dries and a rainbow that comes down over the mockingbird starts the mockingbird cleaning his feathers and as he flies to the power pole stayed 2 hours and continues to preen. The rainbow lifts and dissolved and upon being warm and dry the bird flies away from the first breakfast for another day. And time? Time is just the feeling I knew. Where to be at the right place at the right time and right on the money to observe the first breakfast and the rainbow risen mockingbird. By John Morse

PS. The early sparrow catches the worm do not confuse spirit with internet. The worm after V'ing and S'ing dives back to its hole in the wall. The worm morsels the light of the internet to the special K. The life saving light of the eye of the saviors light if it be Let There Be Light of UC to the shower from the car and the eye is not Pablo Casals damaged eye as it is Easter light that has saved it. The cello is a dived violin with footing on the wall of the internet of the neighborhood special K. And on the mockingbirds first flight he wanted to know what's a cello. And the next morning I took a glass of iced water to the sun and it read the violin will give you the fertility you need not your brothers wish without a gyroscope girl. Which brother are you talking about you have just received the gyroscope girl and the special K.. Why do you have a double entangled belt of cumbersome acknowledgment which I call K? Is that the aura chakra "really" doing it I have told you I lacked when you prayed in church. Papa is it the cummerbund they sing with a peg foot of a cello? No the cello that is an image from the internet I told you not to confuse that and human nature as the fuzzy tail of the squirrel and the mockingbird's nest knows. Happy Easter. To make a man fight his own personality is unrighteousness. Says your cousin the one you thought you would row row row your boat across the rivers to see. She being a precocious siren is making love of your brother at the time because if it's I that made him only marry divorcees then I shouldn't mention fertility of course not to anything except Jesus.. If it's adoption that gave you sons then your sons shall adopt. That is logic. Then was a Son of God born. God is love what is a genealogical young simple game Miley god's infatuation? Aye no I but the butterfly you want to know why? Because the tactile system can be a refresher of the co-ordination by the breeze which the butterfly flies in like the geek to not get lost in like the leaves at least until the powder on the mind is the same as the butterflies wing then which way to go we will leave to updrafts in the breeze praying that you can see and steerage way is more on track like a bee. The born again going through even the past life flashing before his eyes the Pantene Complex is just loneliness beautiful I am as I feel as I remember as I wish I see. Jesus came in rare cases to divide families even by an allegorical sword. That is what I believe evolution truly is. I do not swear by the word allegorical. I wish like all good explorers on the ship through the Mississippi the search for the fountain of youth that I could reverse time as my dream did but when I envy on a romance for the second generation there is a flash preventer in my minds smoked eye.of people, princes princesses or kings middle class, from and held to the past, held to the present Pantene, for the procreations of the futures souls of undetermined experiences and undisguised pride, that so far as I can tell you is a tender non-breaking heart of a skirt tail relationship of the mind and only the reverse in time is a space seat release of slat bar mind trap testimony clearing by the best prophet ever known Easter Himself.. When is the root of jam hernias free love? When after a love dream of this raven beauty and seeing Sudan passing Gaul stones before my eyes to Ghana and a little stronger by gases than I am my jaw on the right side pops back in invisibly and I know it is good like Jason. And when is the root of the gaseous nebula appendix good food like a division of family the sword on Orion's Belt. Man does not eat alone jam when to bless his heart Dean Sterns Tobacco Herbias a five star restaurant where Toni is the chef is how he eats. As sensible as the carbonated drinks that open a Barrett tube. She wants a Duck is what I learn says the raven beauty next door. Shall "I" be Huntington less than sensible or build a cage for a pet window door? I can.be her

Tarzan watermelon StunFowler and. in two's play amore liberal bet.

A thought interjected into a simple sentence is a complex I use the word "duck". Like in the following sentence. Where are the families that What Brian hears Matthew open the. door and lets ducks fly away for, Bless me with my own fertility as much as god blessed us with Jesus Dean? And secures the glass door with a telescope call which wire the web footed friends can't land on seen.

What does the work of courts turning to the right? I only want the word mentions not a fight. The bailiff of a judgement or property managers of lots: adjacent through time of meditation prayer and answer of visa better than com. I think yes and you think no. The judging the nonadjacent lots management. The adjacent lots eating through blessings of love and the heart until proper property is squared an d fair. A previous judgement turn to the right and abba abba loi which seems to be property management's right now A paparazzi's com made people angry throughout time whether numbers apart or close kinship. That is why we use arbitration. Does life really pivot on evolution this morning and something less bad. Like dat teeth isn't that the treatment instead of pressure pot toy let. And a fly into soup as fleeter of feet likewise says Dean for some real appetizers all we had is some croutons dogs. Loosing and gaining wait to be seated for dinner once a day at 5. For the numbers here are not the visa unknown like the neighborhood. Be nice not angry and hush up. Rest up to down your chakra and blind spot eyes in the sprinklers after you have dinner and get a co-ed. Internet friend. Get an age group difference video for your friend and the electricity of the esteem will release to nature.

The next morning the raven beauty drops her egg and and a grasshopper climbs up my chair. And rocks me like an oscillating room that locked me with care. And saved me from a knife fight last night.And at the top post he prays to the sun and looks over at me. I think outside as the tv thinks inn. An equal but nature or man's science equivalent this has been. And which is gods symbiotic thought. For the mockingbird time and I are at a different lot. I might say the con trolls scream and the cricket flies but god in heaven would have a better buy. Inn-door outdoor how complacent they be until nothing is said nothing is known not even a dream for free. I hear the sweep of the homeless from my home and see the greatness of Egypt and even Greece on tv. And the empires stop from speaking hush child hush to charge felony. And a counter felony Is charged who holed my car? It is a clear night and sobering now that the mockingbird is asleep. Two stars shine through a palm tree and they from Jesus can't sleep. And upon the morning can I keep the car and mail in license O Rome do speak. You suggest we take salt and and eat some chips and wash this down with water and ice. Your intention on this cold clear morn am I hearing really good advice? The houses lock has saved me from backstabbing yes that is good advice. But what about the rising sun and the prayer with the grasshopper grace? I am all bent out of shape that is why I am outside in the first place. Red sky at morning grasshopper take warning you are the locusts that Rome won't mourn. Am I to sleep and not to dream I guess I'll have to wake befuddled before born to be alive at the crack of dawn of this machine. I have a lt. Tom micro pin in my butt who is finer of the disabled chair. Navy CG Marine or Air. They used to say when there was Army let Charlie walk with apple on Silverstein sidewalk in Sierra Madre would be d fair. Now my genes from him are similar as with jeans from lt.Tom's gain. A pair from chuck a pair from Tom and up the sun at the crack of dawn. The only problem is chuck didn't rock Tom is country usually classic and both aren't out to date. I only a trainer three of Alexandria barely Christianity but as fine as they come I can see and be and take. "You will come up to me" the mockingbird wondered who said from the cloud in the sun above. Do I make them believe in that voice the birds and the bees with out my son don't suffice. Is His reason the mockingbird or quote the raven which also in a neighboring tree has just sat. Which is sent which is sat and which is dissent advice? Quote the mockingbird the better intended release to the wind a baby under rainbow is my advice. And so young and so old is this pecking game one in black and one in white. That I leave it to Jesus and what I see and sense and moo as my mate and advice. Quoth the raven is just dropping an egg in several days the mockingbird made a better flight. And as my leg heals and the grasshopper receives the rose or the bloody delight if the women are in hell and the men fight. The worm is fed again as the raven leaves and the mockingbirds again alight. And three doves flew to the coast as I woke again and yawned in the sun I think there is some time for toast.

An interception car moved to the rooster to boast. Then the sparrows that Jesus said you are loved more than unheard or chloroformed are fighting or squirm. And why do you have the power to write right or right write?

You ask from the inn tv with all of everything National Geographic to know a former time personal grace. And wonder why I ski lodge with my feat 40 years ago and pick up which we both have as my second generation and can't allow in my face. For the soul wants different you don't have bit the time want different I'll allow my graceless to the time graceful differences of born again. Which birthday does yours count yours country yourselves your child's of time the knowledge of households the knowledge of rhyme. I am to let you exercise your will and strength which exercises my calculations to find the blindness of my possessions so misplacing weak. One is never too old to look or so to speak I am looking at myself and I am getting pretty meek. Three geese circled and then rose and headed out to the west end where west wind blows. And one said see you later and headed to the north south shores to fly with Jonathan Livingston seagull just a Jesus updraft fellow. A home more than a bird is color contrast and word and don't say the gadfly gets addressed. For which fly whisk is white and which fly whisk is black both the same color makes Egypt is back. So this is how you de-command. And where is he and where is I with Jesus or the Muslim race? Read the writing on the wall does it slant in light like Jesus or Mohammed pace? The last s'ing angle worm fed a mockingbird bird Brian what is your plight. Not to know not knows why is my handwriting half far eastern light? I see the light. Why are you unsaid to not see the sites? Rest your head on a tum instead of a bowling blew and pop laugh at aunts. He loves a lemon for a squeeze he says of me. Why don't you call gym's misplaced lighters instead of calling Muslim aunts and ask for gamblers Grant. As if having a Dean Dr Pepper would've suffice to break a leg and it would've when you are laid in the rack six hours before the rooster crows and the clouds discourage l tonight'.

Ahhhh that is a little hypocritical when I mean three knights. And what does the father and son and Holy Ghost say about the nights as I sit totem the right of Roger and watch the baby mockingbird sit on the wall? I have taken my plastic glue shot from Charlie and can't see straight with one eye closed and one so small. So with the spoon in my mouth and Jesus, this isn't the last dinner after all. Shall we stand up and fight and obliterate the worm? Then the roosters crow is over should I ever think of eating lamb. The lambda figure in clouds light is to the ocean to follow the road of incense. Use our cameras our minds our demonstrators and protest the dissent? Time passes the squirrel shows her bushy tail. He eat eggs also how else can he prevail? So I think I'll go back to my rock where there is orchestra rock and rail.. That is after dimmed light and take off of my socks. And in the morning light after having a wet dream I glance at Roger then away can you seed the lot my right leg. Can you see what I see and look a numbered lot as the forgotten? The cornerstone the corner of the lot. Now there are just sprouts of greens that look like stroganoff. And simper fi the gas man refilled a personnel lt. couched allot. The orchestra is coached the birds singing in English lost. Which is more eternal Jesus or Einstein case. As we pull the switch on steams intensity's and figure concentrate and focus electrical sprinkler roast my Charlotte simper fi. And I take a mouthful of corn on the cob a mash a meal and place it on the top of the wall to feed the mockingbirds wail. And I lean into my gyroscope girls breast and a broken leg does heal. A little milk a little cereal for a morning meal.. Praise god more than your icon self with Andrea's breast and as the Zendacar prevails. Your eyes will be uplifted to a place where there isn't this darkness tongue. Ahhh is my lung more precious than my loin? Ask the nurse her priorities and keep them clean and we'll feed and sharpen the light thread pipe of your Roman waisted groins machine. Just to Jesus a few days before an earthworm went into a wild satanic writhing. Late that night as I feel that I was chess clocked I relieved myself and peed out what looked like a four inch tape worm. The mockingbirds were scared that the devil had gotten into their food but we had previously buddied up heart to heart and I reassured them we had had come from a good brood. So this is Sunday and I wonder how Jesus didn't break his legs on the cross. The son has risen so has peep who last night ate cherry Baum. Paradise is a beautiful site and it can hurt in contrast color as the fathers rainbow gift it isn't lost. What in storm is the reign to rebalance nature tossed? A little time a little Jesus and a father who is rainbow boss. Oh Abraham I am relieved from putting my right foot in put my right foot out turn it all around and shake it all about the devils knight of my brain and foot by knowing slipped disc I am flying to Ghana past midnight. To save from stroke my brain which hadn't until landing seen the person of anger hidden between boiling templates of memory to only be lucid when co- vid seen never or die. Then peep with rainbow past alights this clear dawn sunny day sunny side up delights on the host a telephone IT wire and re- Peter post. My pelvis is weak because my right leg is lame the only way I can recompense is to use the shoulders below my brain. So demonstrate, March and bust ye hearty stroke nullified as it lays my heads they're (now I lay me down to sleep) is still the peep of the hummingbird and the lilac as I eat my jam and bread. I don't fly off the handle instead. It will be a long uphill road and flight and there will be times in the middle where you will serve and move from trials and right or wrong but eventually the flight levels Out except on a rock like the Hudson River Sully which sits high and levels In and Out and one reaches a comfortable plateau: or this earth and heaven and country isn't working in God's sight. Do you think or love? I think therefore I am cannot beat God is love. Samuel said "if tomorrow is like yesterday then today is Friday" TGIF. Is that how time reverses as of the dream and real time of Easter? And what is last days time ? Is it a continuous Easter for the Christians with the real-time of the messiah an amazing son of god incredible soul strength and prince of peace, his kingdom appearances solid state with his majority believers so the earth can have a new 1000 year contract? Mescal Beseech (I am in the clap of thunder) and Avenged put them in the fire and watch them go Jesus included what a tow, Mescal Beseech and Avenged.. At the beginning of Jesus time He emanated and Cyrus later released the Jews. We saw a more glorious Him than you ever dreamed of Nebulous, see His water and air conditioning and fire department to put out the flames and cool by thunder. Don't go down the tubes of food for thought but laxative like loose weight and be bluff. Don't make your bed to bend you out of shape it hurts as a shark without a diamond promise and that can be a waste. Jesus be with you so is the flu! More than a mouthful is a waist. The leaves of souls go up the leaves of souls don't stay up and go down as everything is radio active and stereo from left to sounds right sounds and around. Steer by both ears with right stereo sound and your eyes will work an impulse route and careful with the end of patience and flu aye will be sober and sound. If your eyes see double try your right stereo patience horn and look the full moon in the eye. Electric mummification shock does wonders to empty the gas.

If my love for the younger generation is a fake then the Bible needs new names or does not include fiction. God is love.

God in my experience came from a dream I had as a child. I in my self and mind was in a large all soul enveloping circle spinning around and around with the center visible and at the same time as the wheel was spinning the center or hub was moving closer then farther away then close to me again. From that dream I later felt I could do out of body back flips of what I was in reality to the spinning wheel dream (a galaxy) but I could never bring myself to complete the flip because I feared I would disappear from the wheel totally and perhaps never never again re-appear. Later in life this manifested itself in my life as straight A',s and the deans honor list in my sophomore year at UCI and then being lost in a out of body dream to a nuclear reactor and never knowing quite what direction I should take through school and life. Recently I have taken a writers worksop where the instructor mentioned that my "poetry" goes around like in a circle comes up with something new but then just goes around in a circle again. As the course ended he recommended reading Ulysses by James Joyce and thought my work was similar in intent a kind of stream of consciousness style. I 4 months later I am remembering his comment and visualizing my ancient childhood dream of the spinning wheel. I can see the dream now that I had in junior hi lol in my room as I am writing this.

My question is: is my love a fake a fiction to the Bible as a reversing stare a stereo of sound and beauty illusion of eye acknowledgment of location where one side is actually the other, left is right and right is left. (Here is another "duck") (From nicotine to wine.with Spinzer and the Internet catching what is left of your balance the ups and downs the left and right the in and out, until in the waist chakra and therefore heart of a raven haired beauty lmao (like may account owe) sighting over the garden wall growing two inches a beauty of a flowering neighborhood of silent majority secrecy and first knowing where in the galaxy you are.). It depends on what aye found because what I found was Is-real.

I found besides seeing double airplanes as eye disorientation I had power from an ear disorientation on the ground that may have been intentional man made by cable in my room followed by body biology into eyesight. When what you are hearing from the left is really from the right is the eye powerful or are the heavens opening up closing the personal sight not drunkenness of one airplane to put heavens reality to two places at once two airplanes as quickly as a wink of the Saint Nick eye who can go down chimneys or what is smoke doing with biblical wine? Candy is dandy but liquor is quicker Santa Claus. The only way to support my heart is with like of the Flojos of sole. Sadly, bullishly and not truly Hitchcock is hung to rudely be sir up how sweet it is with Pantene women with the soul that is not in Emery's image anymore as his laments have been ruled out. When I get angry I mean Sgt. Peppers soul changing and role changing dealing home.

And my right foot warms in the sun. I should lead with my right foot if I wish balance again and a gyroscope girls flojos body gifts. Did aye say gyroscope she wonders what she is if not dealing the role of being a woman to me and it is I that doesn't balance like the bird I see flying in my face with wings of a shadow is-real and the word. Bee that to me and I see only flowers really father of high dam time. To mature and grow Jesus updates for only a year will be Jupiter and Venus is aligning in the palm trees to the moon and we be with god to break the age rule. The earth time in carbon dating, the fourth dimension time itself, the time it takes to walk in the morning on four legs walk at midday on two and walk in the evening on three? Is time more than an orbit? Is it all time of the past present and future. Is it only mankind's time of peace not the last days of the daze of stroke and war. TGIF.

The bull sits in a rut in his garden and wishes to move as the earth did first, General Fernando is the name of wire received and new phone on order kiss. And as I and the sun rise I see my aura and am told by Matthew that some count tribally and mentions the Sikhs and Hindu belief of aura. O Leona this home does move so take a gander as you sit and serve. Wired in the refrigerator and wire to the phone. I know no number but the social K. So in the shadow and is-real and wordless power it is time for breakfast oats banana cider not a curd. Why does the India marine wake to a good mood while the mother tends her lot in a tender loving word. She tends the home not every morning is an Easter and a catty bird. whether the son is a sun rising chakra aura the son is risen however long. He must be clean and organized and have a better phone pole of a home then than your wordlessly room. She understands the pipe as ungodly fire not the good mood sunrise of either faith brood. You think the morning and son and poetry is a disgrace and like to tear paper tiger tails in my face.

Mr Hitchcock Who will foot the bill? The one whose lame foot is grafted to the raven haired beauty's foot and ankle to pray with her instead of the unseen dirt and tobacco at my feet I have foolishly called the monsters eye. It is a graft of gravity of mankind or heaven. The gravity of a cop graft has led me pulling my leg in the wrong but penniless way before a vision I had of swimming under old hulls of boats and a rose garden how is this connected to war? How much war time must repeat itself before we find ourselves from first time a fish. That crawled onto land to become the first woman and man that ate from a dish to the skies they call rose microwave.my toast. Aye no I but I I'll have my garden toast and jam from a 110 toaster strudels off the floor my boast of my feet my breakfast be my sweet house mother in my neighborhood awe. Meh Hitchcock as you socked me last night I have grown a chest bone posture becoming upright. Is war some graft of defiance as are cops of arrogance? Maybe Miss Achilles will answer before a fortnight. If she does not love me she does not kiss. If she likes me and knows my reasons and heart then I will relax.I do believe Jesus healed the harm in my foot and let the lame walk should I throw a farthing to a church a microwave toast or hull just to live in dreamland bliss. Aye yes I but don't retract my wings O of is-real bird I hear them sing. Is she only charms of knowing keeping several from harm I think the lord can do as well. After all it is up to man and me to organize and clean up my smell. There is a lock to the "left right"," right left"and it is In ones bowels.

Does the milk spoil as it is left out? Yes it does with time that is wrong that is set to what matters is the destruction in war is what is left. And what matters during or after the war is an answer to a problem that is right. Hold these times together in your strength of yourself and you have a bend. Silly tiger bends are not right angles they are heartbreaking and sometimes are released through only the laxative as an old man who rightfully has an intelligent idea and can with childhoods time accept the will of god to maintain the supply line of prosperity. For Him and man are to be suppled Constitutional rights of separation of church and state I will spread my internet acquaintances to Venezuela and not hesitate.

Fore there is the beautiful Fabi Molina and usually again I wake in the morning sun to good brood poetry not this neighborhood debate of made in the USA or raven haired beauty made honors and Fabi is to not be made n the USA. Isn't it enough to have one heart broken to see a young man fall in love at first sight to be banished to have ones weak chin abruptly brought out of his chest by being socked told it was wrong to love. This before I have more of an upright heart on the ribs of my chest seem to move like ingrown hairs of my face to be little shivered out of the jaw of my heart. A weak jaw turned into heart rib pride. Is someone a black overshadowing flag of Socked to my body at midnight a blow from is-real shadow wing and timing power.telling me Miley god's infatuation is a dam that will break? It broke my heart to have the weak jaw love of a raven haired beauty rights in sight banished but with a bigger heart and given up to heaven the raven which is a bird more powerful than the mockingbird. In all fairness to trial and error Tarzan Stun fowler he is now flirting with a blonde. Why trial and error because this seems more evolution than god creating an Adam Eve situation from the underwater rose garden of medication having more law rights than meditation of self expression. So I stand stronger and with a bigger chest but less of a little heart.And what in maddening heat wakes at night so cool. A mockingbird sings His delight and a downy t-shirt. covers Cupid's wound..Money talks big bucks lock and tomorrow's prosperity is today's effort and grade. Pride Tomorrow and dowery your aye will get a new gift from my family and on the plateau's t-shirt it will speak and adorn.This feeds my soul and again my heart will be open and reborn.

By John Morse

TWO SUNS FOUR POLITICAL PARTIES

*T*he molecule that movingly is ahead of the problem of spacemen, chastising of subconscious flight. The furthest reach is the only one available an infinite light. So the shorter ones don't count as much a human a light. If I am the enlightened light at two places and between them transport transfer or commute by weight then I am the energy of the second suns light. And be that my business credit ability and history in genetic foresight, I am the leading option to use for procreation. Double the socialization enlightenment of double standards of two places and both sons standards, leading or trailing, when the transfer of and by both is finished: "because once business is over and the commute done do I have two areas of enlightened light or one?" in other words the life of the party between two suns is the transfer between them with one sun light being seen by the other one is questionable after the transfer. The lights dancing in the eyes for a time, when darkness overshadowed my friends salvation lifeline. A second hand on a watch in black light, tunnel between 1 and 3, l and REM not.

Mindfulness and meditation, through sudden waking by stress though a Leo Kottke essence of frustration overcoming fill em time, the hand on the head side reclining lessens chaos and pressure like the sealed bottle of time a soul, thought, are one in the same.

That is for Sunday bless their hearts. When the chest is filled then the stomach usually wants treats to eat. When on a glide slope to you Huntington Beach finding the alternate doctor sheens's office apart from John Wayne is airport,, I am loved to fill a vacant heart and made more than leased as she is Mary not beer. And blessed by love a power of the lord there are many that eat there with good friend Darlene, and be guided by icon GPS glide slope freeway Elaine. It is in twos the alternate freeways and their lanes are giving and receiving. What is the loin or lain the freeways, the more the merrier? The squeaky wheel gets greased? The talk'o are more noise of frustration, fries I will be mindfulness, and therefore meditation tonight be prepared to sleep.

In a hidden complex the good tooth is fairly bouncing. not-not the dentist straightens my neck not turkey but raven in the chair waiting. Hurry sir John, hurry. Carpe Diem. For the molecule like the buzz which is like a bee in the ear faster than a speeding flight is ahead by car of her by 48 hours and if you delay any further it will not only find you but will make its Name mark. So we sit in bouncing pond delusion with Father Time's only dream of knots end not ending from their beginning and we see peer Torrents tears eat at the dining room table in sea pier Torrents ocean's everlasting, moving time. Why don't you make p pop a chess piece as a dentist and I'd play the game. Move time the opened art stops like a flopper stopper to be rushed to the dentist. Blocked the blessing, stopped by beaus, through temple in the ear, at the dentist and there, from prehistoric in my heaven meant at church, to help the time of there and your teeth, and relax and hear.. I have seen "The Hornets Nest " too often and have some PTSD. Do you know the true flopper stoppers of time? Santa Claus is coming to town pls the saints be praised. By John Why don't Morse.

Thoughts don't wash them up Kings do. Is time governed by minds eye or heart? I have seen dinosaurs in church that screeched at the microphone. Is it what god sees in us and we see in him or is it what we feel of him and what he feels of us? I see the Greek chair the chair noble and I sit in it, I see it and I feel it. It has an outside and life time. The "idea" of the Greek chair has unlimited coherent limits of time, outside two inside as long as man will be made in the image of the sides of god's time. He is a man that can by bracing his weight and wait upon the floor be constructed like the Grand Canyon by time. If this idea is in thee heavens say "The Greek chair is floating in the space station."I see and feel that you are an airman that has had half his chest blown away. The pork barrel rolls vapor trails on edge. Will the surgeon operate from the space station?" So you see king Giuseppe it is as much as you see and as much as you feel that is what the heaven's bare for Yahweh, wait weight of the "thought" whose use it is proclaimed is eternal. Eternity fits my definition of time. Is it that your minds eye and mine to gods minds eye thoughts of two, three, or four times (dimensions) are of time? If the thoughts wash up they get cleaner on one hand and militarily if we include Rome with the galaxy parties turning on pi 's didn't graduate, they are washed up.

Their chair rights are taken from them because the uplift from the sponsors work is not theirs. Move damn it and try again, somewhere over the rainbow though it not be more than rain should it be a new county clover. The Kings graduate, they must be to be kings. There are four/four political parties or moar two times of light spinning the photons. Eternity within a universe creation without measuring tampering and what man bares to instruct a constructive gravity chair to floor chair to Grand Canyon to peace beyond fission to exclude the entropy maintenance repairs of (quantum physics) measured tampered by pi is the chosen one. As Lisa would simply say "know". As Emille would respond to "neutron of Higgs Boson, particle of god, feather from tendon, muscle from bone, a dinosaur's god maybe not, the molecule is and is not-not sew to be got."

There are two or more times to the universe theorizes John. So for every sun that is different a different speed of light. Per one speed of light there is a heaven and hell and two political parties. Per two speeds of light twice as many. We have a know see um space surgeon party wrapped in subliminal space, and a knowledgeable particle of god party welcome to the Xmas seasons feasts, a dichromatic eye space party that changes colors as the dimensions approach the speed of light. a universal dialectic party that can hear songs just by sitting on the desert. If there was a man with there was a chair, and beyond the edge CD is not that chair, Chernobyl but baby universe is a chair, and pi is their right to start insanity of not saving your soul or having appropriate good luck, then what turns a galaxy around but the clocks of Gogol and the universe of parties delight? Seat Adam and seat Eve from another circle that seats at a higher light. And make politics more like as many parties as the thoughts wash up upon thee shore as the Kings do. And wash up His opponent's men. That is for a time.

A Kings rule unless golden, or of God and recorded like the Grand Canyon records geological time should only be a man's measuring not tampering that turns pi's court in and so doing does not TAMPER a King of Kings proclamations. A Yahweh may make the photons spin around the neutrons at different speeds in sight as a news department as pop centered in space patrol light. When the Kings proclamation is plural as is the photons count of his subjects and not singular: between God and himself: the proclamation is plural poo usually tampered, hung to gravity of the clouds per adjective adverb which pluralizes the singular noun and verb. day by sunrise to until the time of the Kings court (the earth turns) to plurality of randomness. Measured, tamper me not know more, I see through my electron microscope of Yahweh two photons where there once was one, no more. And tampering not the kings proclamations he is of and between himself and god and remains not know more than not more than one more within the walls of the Will; that which holds from within the Maine not tzar. How good it is to hear aviation roar but timeless like a peace of this earth a Grand Canyon rivered not Ruhr a piece of four leafed clover in the reign dew soil, a shamrock it is not but who will cut the layers of time through parsley sage titanium, aluminum anodized, and thyme? Lord are you not with persons employed more to reign and rain for the earth, which I don't disdain. But the atmospheric rivers are on below, His hand so what cuts from above from flesh and lamb eww through the river-folds of titanium and land. Life from rain be the last frontier. The clover is more at the end of time, than rhyme and sooth of titanium mine. Next in line for reign my god, this diamonds place inevitable upside down to teas tees space. And there is no moth for the light of the new enlightenment, reading is done on computers not books is my lament.

BREAKING LOOSE

AN UNDERDOG TWIN

*I*f it is in your conscience or what you hold as personal from a time that was splendid like the formation of your personality from childhood to present and there is a crisis or rather trauma that stirs you for answers do you look to yourself afterward for the memory of that word conscience? Can you stand in a church and feel other believers hearts that are broken so that together your heart hurts? Once asked for that to be remembered is it in your soul or have you processed too many refresh or camera clicks on the machine you are telling us to coincide. The brain wall. Holding everything mysterious of life's ecosystem say living of spirit and evolving wise inside either wide as a Saint Nick or pregnancy or flat and hard as an abdominal perfect. Wait until you become apparent as a human and break the Gordian Knot, in other words mature. Do you breathe with that even the first breath you take. Does it support your heart cavity where you first feel love here or hear lost chatter and static of kitten foreign alien music?

Historically an architect and lawyer of structures engineering. and city planning or social ecology an anthropology. Let it all hang out they say..Two abdomens of twins made in love these walls do not have space except to break one another's "kingdom" as not to tie the birth or marriage bond each as individuals twin's lucky stars. We weren't a culture of majority rights of twins in birth or marriage until recent Supreme Court decisions giving rights to wellness of the mind. If the twins are not from one star indivisible, but divisible as something in space you could say an incredible instability mass wraps the one light into two tails which over time have two tales of bees and wasps. Luminous moon quality for one and shine as a star for the other.

In the beginning we went to the moon now we are going to the star of bee. Do they not enter into the same heavens? "Yes in spaciness but who says the earth and the world heavens holds the fourth dimension of time. By the walls of the fetus they are saved. By your faith you are saved said Jesus. Sorry who is this by your faith in walls you are saved? As the hypothesis we are civilization earth or uncivilization space, with walls or without walls on earth or in space. Which of the twins is saved and which calls for hallelujah TGIF as innocent for the real time to be what thou bee saved, as the shade on my face changes time by minutes one month from six months a year.

Roman jail walls do shake and then brake upon earthquakes leading to the rights of the instability space mass to match the salvation byTGIF. If I cry I'll say goodbye to T to when if it is eternal as I am nosing around.." What is this feeling an illusion of the perfection of a butterfly landing on flowers in the garden in full bloom of seated rise from a beautiful daughter. I Design and beauty is it my salvation? Jesus said your faith is your salvation.

My mother in a dream appeared between the walls in the door and talked to me as if she were in her forties. Those years I had driven a steep road and fallen perpetually to one side. She forgot healing me to go back to school and get her counseling degree. I grew bitter and drove that steep road again as an exit from her state California to the north is and as all I knew. She said in the dream "I don't love you you know" I quickly rationalizing said "I do love you." Then in the new northern state I realized what the thousands of words her real love and curse on me as more I than only a play on words for my ability had come to me from afar. But it wasn't her ability's in the north where I had similar and haunting weird misconceptions and those were the words massive and spinning in front of me "never to graduate."

I had a tendency she said to be flippant and thereby reject good ideas cutting off my own nose she would slyly remark with plenty of good things laid on my table. Such things as tamale pie with corn.and the shop where we could use tools. She gave me ravens and hated hawks. The ravens are "basically"which is a sic word I heard, thinking as a tough and scavenging species like a goat and our family dog that eats trash. Those that eat eggs in the trash is compost are anti my ability of taste. I think she would agree with that.

I have found more work in restaurants than dogged by counselors that say same old same old as the exit policy or no escape. This exit belongs to and for long lasting blackbirds that eternally explore but fight themselves for the dominance of a crowning achievement in the line up of life. The civilized of birds protected their eggs in a nest. In the north there were plenty of eagles and hawks and falcons.

One falcon is Did the other is Do. Do follows Did to find out what life is like in a hierarchy's skies are torn. Together they are Didlydo but only Did has done enough to enter heaven no matter how hard Do tries. How righteous literally asks the Indian and for Do how long a space time? Do they each house a different department house in departments of idly different time personalities. Did is making a baby from his mate. Do is making Friday revolution time with her baby for a mate. The entrance and point of the two abdominal walls is to get one to do something for the other isn't it a state university student compared to university of state student and both compared to an Ivy League family. Is this in seal creation (walls) (eggs in nests or from chickens) by the will and 4design of God.. of graduated students?

Break the seal of knowledge and go back in time and feel the beaten sandman body and how it is sloped down and sloped sideways for a Friday on a bed until recovery's postures conscience when? Then will you fill in the cracks in the sidewalk with the souls of your feat of friends that walk with you now and with yourself the balance of drop foot becomes in spirit debate the spine strengthening as warriors of the knowledge seal discuss the walls of doors. Say design (flowers) rules over survival of the fittest evolution. Yes and that is admirable but not proven and therefore not allowed on curriculum as of today. As of the day remarks of genetic man does design and build have hopping ghost and protective history revolution?

Can corn genes hop between different types of corn and genetically change the plants which are involved? Yes they can. Can I have a baby as well as adopt? Yes I can. Does this limit me to believing the adopted of one year and three days older (Camaro Jim Dandy to the rescue) is partially a corn gene hopping genes spirit flushed into flesh and blood of {Mrs. tin Lizzie.of Corona) my mother, good leg from Jim a priority before having a baby me and me is what I nicknamed the universe. This includes her much more in my thoughts than my dreams of the frontier days as we explored the Indian cultures on family vacations. My mother as far as I know answered yes.

My father said this when I was a child at the dinner table "John is just filling in his hollow leg." It was the right leg that was hollow. Does Freud in certain cases make the lame walk like Jesus did?

Yes. In the halls of intermediate school I joked with a school mate about which of us had a trick knee.

As for I? Do we need Friday as a revolution more than present times and terms of history? Maybe. And I am to redeem my soul seeing the answer in front of the doors to my church to my eyes of the kaleidoscope we call metropolis.

Not always there are other states to visit Believing the Father gardens the vineyard so that the grapes stay with similar brethren. Conscience of.posture medicinal revolution is even better late than a never dream or crashed or Friday revolution.

With design those beautiful abdominal walls become posture conscience depends on time of maturity or of time rebuilt; or time of the Holy Ghost acceptance. Samuel once said "If yesterday was tomorrow today would be Friday" Paint yourself out of a corner. Esteem a way out of a corner the corner market your brother did have the rights to and you didn't. From the bikini land down under with that peeking to the top of thunder.

Patty and I were talking about countless moons ago of Knight and Snow White overnight feelings not recognized as engagement but going far enough as days passed into night to paint Patty's choice rights into a corner. Patty is also a do, not really a did yet. Do was due overnight but made the DEW line flight just barely when one of those dids her band boyfriend entered what she was supposed to didlydo. I left and I went from bottomless to a solo drift into the bottomless space a vacancy of the angels and heaven in a happy but unlit candlelight night. Then from that night and seven days I found rest and soothing heart the place with rev. I Moon. The thunder from His church entered my heart space. I got a job at the ski lodge cooking.

We lived with that from the past for the future into the present. In our hearts I in heaven, our rights of living not much more torn asunder, We don't realize the past ancient history and modernization the differentiations days. The earth if you sit on a north south line dips rapidly changing the sun on my face to shadows of leaves on my face as different time minutes every day those ways for a month every six months as the seasons change and therefore the time of sunsets and sunrise. The rotation for 12 months is from the east to the west.

Hemispheric cats and dogs of owners that had a kitten and puppy love are best for housing for what we plan as native innocents hoping for and dream and blunder. I mean let me add a thought to say what Samuel said from LA "If yesterday was tomorrow today would be Friday." It takes time therefore it is time of Friday Saturday and Sunday rightfully if time takes you back to yesterday..Do lives does he have the ability to helicopter on the ski slopes with remembrance of the earth nswe each ski season a year flying like only a skiing helicopter can? He understands when life's trials are enough with release of tension by sport. to use an old fashioned word 8 to 5 or "to much" like "I can't take it anymore", If it is to much by Friday morning to work on thru the week then by Samuel we go skiing. As one senior Did said from LA "banal and I'm going swimming " oh blight on me for thinking the senior was talking about myself when he was actually only explaining Samuel.

A tin Lizzie driving Colorado native said "Jim dandy to the rescue Jim dandy to the rescue go Jim dandy go" That is until he found every day a Friday with retirement until the last days becalmed became a fact. Well last days thinking you say if today is yesterday there is no tomorrow..

The Wall door that dreaming only a mother of mother or mate or person of help and counseling of job opportunity can find a door to open. That is if they ever can with the last days. Remember AI rather than the refresh click on a machine what makes history that can be reasserted is a conscience. Thunder,,thunder, and waiting. time that is in my heart, that is all of the infinite of the change which can be loved good when in the future if there is room for the mistakes of from the past and the last days catches you first then the door is open. The future going north western finding ms Berg and a life of my own.

For your health and safety insists mom come back. For my own health to be under the Stars and Stripes my brother was serving Patty came back and we are cautious of strangers. For history or to present future revolution?. That is if I am in a pathos cycle which I presume can be worked out by slaloming. Where I feel repetition being worked,' remodeled in my mind, beauty and the precision amongst others until that practice becomes habit to define my self identity. It does open the door to the Winter Olympics to ski. Which will be true to history oh AI for the wall and door of the ski lodge of the mountains? The door of skiing It is only your time of maturity not your maturity of time which can fix falling to one side. How do I make time in the long run: become an old man as wise as the hills?

I heard you Samuel whisper "don't go home but if I tell you to get help from Patty she mainly remembers your clarinet song and you might go back to Egypt and the coffee shop but the pastrami you have eaten here you will remember". Which time and which block neighbored wall you do wail like an.air raid siren Samuel if I go back and like a field lieutenant here you do brother. The see of tear brown birds. Oh they are all wailing there is so much confusion in the sees at the Holiday Inn when Grandma died that there is no time in the eagles but instead the ravens where to if you have time you return to removes the Saint John's Wart out of you until Jesus has Christmas. The air damsels telephoning will be remove peace from you by telemarketing rather than a debate with water or eating your supper in peace. Be that stay here.

And I am thinking like a donut hole and the pastrami sandwich sank to into four on the floor when Patty said, "sit with me up and make body contact lo is and the child my sister will go upstairs. The posture conscience is it a confused plastics brain camera over sandman time? It can be helped. How are the Denver omelettes tasting on a greyhound bus stop between here and California ? John this is the see the writing out the door and upwards that started this journey does it end the same? What the revelation has is time to reveal as is the skies are appointed but by the limits of the limitless. There are checks and balances to our political system we are elect with election that counts." Is that a bridge a truth is that true? Climb with me in the mountains oh AI because the lower plains and their valleys have called me their anti. I loth O'Mara good morning! Then I heard that whisper again " if you loose conscience of your grandmother it will weaken your spine out, if you loose your conscience of Patty you will loose your heart and your mind by thunder and the beautiful in the sky.

But it is to you true that times limitless skies are torn doesn't eternally make the earth go around on a two years of skiing." I sat with her at the Holiday Inn and had one cup of coffee. I couldn't quite have the ability with my cousins living in Idaho to hold her to a home she came from in my name which she with all my heart deserved. I walked with her hand in hand to Saint John Catholic Church and spent the last dollar I had and took a taxi to the airport for a flight to LA.

A man on the airplane drew a symbol for me. It was an upside down T with a V resting on the bar with two dots inside the V. It was I falling head over heals for my heart it was separated and silenced as I was slid to four-seats behind because time love trust and adventure of destiny thwarts (as canoe thwarts are structural members) eternity as evolutionary had ended. Was it from thunder from Rev. Moon in my heart and Peter in Patty's? Was it the last days of ATT before breakup? It was a day remembrance of the day I had walked to a shop and bought a gold ring for myself and the return to Idaho when that if eternally for myself became possible. Possible! I wanted Patty to visit Southern California and I told her our family had a boat and we could take her to Catalina island. There was a yacht on a trailer justifying the sea parked next to the ski shop when I had passed stoically silently in the back seat of the taxi.

Runway speed up and full throttle into the sky and I left my heart in Boise Idaho on the cross hill with the fan jets of Boise Cascade idling for a run and near falls to the Grand Canyon..What else is left for the peregrine falcon pair when ages of skies part? Why her belief in Seattle more than her home here in Idaho? Where I toured with Rev. Moon in Seattle even in the wrong district which ended low in a cat house. Was there not a root moonbeams to her faith? She said for herself she always was up against a solid wall that she couldn't get through. There was a small kitchen when she invited me to brunch breakfast and I her mother and father were invited. I was remembering my out of body dreaming that without maturity of time and concentration and conscious focus couldn't keep what myself in the dream was the thought there and return. She was similar genes in her mind we both wore blue jeans. The door was there for me so to see the slalom gates the supply room entrance but as my mate Patty my jobs opportunities make that kitchen just a foreboding solid wall for her feeling there would be no real door of prosperity, a house John and a ring? And a church to open the door and see all the people. There was no door to open for her. Where do out of body dreams lead when you stay in the time of the dream? I was born that way and by our serendipity meeting as the inventors say it runs in families. My father said I came by that legally, I am a Morse code she is a Berg "cold hands warm heart".. Where would she put the child? Up to the Lord? There was a dim remembrance of the ski lodge kitchen there was a locker door that open gave me interpretations of eternity of time and falling.

This was new and partially an old answer to her exploring with me, It wasn't the old feeling of out of body cultural shock like I had in Africa.. When I flew in jets I felt like I was in the pilots eye command chairing. I wanted more time to give her this feeling. Then my T on borrowed time ran out? She felt helplessness frustration and despair and several severe days felt she shouldn't live. The Jesus boy in a mosaic holding a carpenters square in a catholic monastery retreat helped. Found in the borderline between the two cities helped. Yes An extra Van Gough on starry nights by rev. Moon. That helped. A last hot fudge sundae at a diner after she had Sadie Hawkins like taken a me out to a play helped. She said "I hope you enjoy this because it cost me a lot of hard earned money."

Two in the afternoon at LAX my father walked down the boarding aisle and greeted me with a huge smile and a big hug.

Had I bought the boat in Idaho making the purchase of our third yacht possible? My mother said if you are a pilot you will only marry your airplane. Yes but I am only know a.pilot a private pilot. If I got a job first with a door in the wall even though I dream to tend that the door is a dream reality I am born that way that Patty did see. Until then I will just hole up in a monastery and the door will open to the faxes of Idaho for the writing on my doorknob and Patty the upstairs key. A song played in my ears from the past my block of memory freed and the faxes, the Friday down or the pastrami up, ages long ago opening is what from here I pray. And sea with one brother and sing with the other until I see the corn growth on my feet planting the corn field door of fax opportunity and telephone pole tree farm for Mountain bell or family and friends. If I adopt will you save one for me? If you are a woman of influence. You must be and I am dreaming again with you my second mother, and first power of snow and tree and knight. The nuns gave grandma the Iglesias and me a pipe, paper, and food, shelter, clothing, brotherhood and nun.

The third boat went to my brother of the sea. The song precious moments went to my brother of song. All on a trick from MCI family and friends when all the Bells were anti-trusted and broken up into smaller companies. They strung a wire from Chicago to Idaho and my Morse family bible was stolen. All legally left was my address book and that looked like It had been mauled. I received one bible from my cousins to help. The fault is the time between earthquakes of the California earth rare so et tu MCI be the way and light of credibility that the real stronghold is open to be seen. A rarity and job opportunity doors may be found and dude in Orange County. It is a rarity that Caltech counts in Newport more than a boat and song. What they like to credit is cars much like business jets not amusement rarity to old time distance and clunky cars a tin Lizzie. Jim dandy to the rescue? Not really near homeless time. Except for the women in golden brand new day shorts standing against the homeless neighbors wall as a gene hop potential and too corny Jim.

Newport on Friday they May bless you with a root beer float. Coo coo ahh choo mrs.u u U up Jesus loves you more than you will no.

By John Morse

THE BANTERED CANTER

What me understand? I learn therefore I like: day or night, like a branch from my right toe dancing along the Milky Way and tell me my type is it involved as the branch from my eyes whether both sides of the clouds from day or magical in the see thru night. You can hear only two ears instead of four except to ignore a rule or break the no in your head you hear and climb to a higher union universeSearching the /diadems that lay on your head while laying on your cones front, vertebrae straightened out rising to a filling be moon, hushed by neighbors which are of arching types of ghosts ascendency in my ears and eyes. The broken or ignored rule outside hearing seeing no. I will obey when you cry, defining the architecture ecology ascendency of current time to wit of all love of neighbors within a city- state of architecture insides to outdoors sides with God's time in one mental freeze frame images. The right side of time. A midnight apparition then came to me and filled myself with thoughts so scary. The right side of my legs not the star in my back and you won't walk with four legged laser monsters bipedal. as your. Thyrsus Fertility to you and fertility to me a man called horse. I have found where my teeth were by spit even though they bacterial Johnny like decayed like our galaxy that is moderately old. Meant as for an eye and a tooth not got but passed to each other's: an eye For an eye a tooth For a tooth my cat. Acid rain is an industrial revolution excuse to not be eye, not be it is the son that wakens since birth with the sun cogito ergo sum and has not lost virgo hood by natural succession. I see branches coming to from my toe after the neighbors tree was trimmed, tripping to Ralphs in the Black Light in am. Alex Haley says roots not branches. Then the next night by heavens standard, I went to the car no shocking appearance the horsemen cantered, put a soothing solution in my eyes not slandered, and heard the innocence of a kitten bantered, all the horsemen ceased their cadence lanterned, and realization justly entered might that if I have a catharsis supplanted, the thoughts flowing to my head so slanted, from only a kitten purring reality of a living midnight muse recurring. A tiger living in the eye of god, cat and me from the garden so seeing, Meow-glee the snake from still to sinking, cat and me till of age just soda drinking. then just the genes of my heart supplanted, slinking snake no longer planted. Then it came to me in my hand beholden, a cigarette lighter that flame not touch tobacco but only candle be token. And how can this not be his true, as I have dished the lunch not Rhine, of orange from beak of ip raven, a grape vine in minds eye, but penicillin for infection beau. A different slant of light from sun and moon, cracks in the sidewalk peaking from the corner disastrous into my room. Milky Way just a candy dandy like a fig branch from my toe, blind eye black holed galaxy or infected beau? A deadwood backdrop snake says you. Watch and merry my infectious raven, indulge my eyes but not marry my subconscious only penicillin, for what is the ages of or man from uncle help, you have from McCallum the Dickinson been whelped. Love if merry may put pains in your back, to tip the ball and jacks of gene choice cherry, then in your heart which with this eternity supplanted, opens from many to one to Mary, and this is how wings grow and you may fly into the one to carry. I found it, eye lost it, eye found it, from the heavens to the hand typing. I is you. If I say I do come down over you man, I mean you do come down over me. It is command language logic. The match of this command logic is IE "I only seem capable of writing with bush hedge and thing. Factually I am a little man but I do get my ire up in creative piece to write and in escape to cemeteries to control fortunate families." Knowing yourself for one half (I do get my ire up in creative peace) and knowing your opponent for the other half (the escape to cemeteries to control fortunate families) reverses the command by putting the ball in the others court in the same command. You is I. It is a confrontation undertaking and or is the cloud coming down to my hand in a space of time over night understanding. (Bushes, Hedge and Neighbored Neighbored Spirit.).

By John Morse

SPACE BABY

*T*ames I will quote part of your paper for a moment. "He who is filled with profound yearning for nature, who seeks everything in nature and is, in a manner of speaking, a sensitive instrument of its secret action, will take for his teacher only the man who speaks of her with worship and faith." What is war? Eminent domain too the Roman coliseum, too the teacher of worship and faith?

One breath takes insides and out. What is it when that is lost except to nature? All of "space" time.? Einstein I quote "If you buy the notion that reality consists of the things in your freeze-frame mental image right now and if you agree that your now is no more valid than the now of someone located far away is space who can move freely, then reality encompasses all of the events in spacetime." War is the hell of the sun turned to microwave heat reality which translocates the spirit to here now and then only until baptized by a water sports nipple bottle being poured on your head. Nature remises. The reality by far and large is Newtonian and Electricity, be the haughty skin stretches taught in the heat of the sun its only cool reality the goosebumps in the sun. The point being is Eine beyond reality is a type of neuron-sport. With peace there is bread to eat be it with only the birds and dawn or enclosure. Without a man and animal absolutely, totally, zero, nothing would be as one, anything, anywhere, everywhere because there would be no known. That sounds like a loss. Like the man who speaks of her with worship and faith is a win. There can be "Hen Ek Doin" with Aristophanes arm in arm with the father enjoying the Newtonian plants. It is fall now and time for rain, cooling heads so they can be merry Mary whose next daughter I have just economically foothold and seen. She is responding to the vertical and lateral forces; spectacles, testicles, wallet and watch. Realness with my grace and walk of Lou Gehrig as my optical illusion the jewel plants in enlarged glasses. Which came first? Uranium, the tree, or feeding the masses by flambeau Cameroon's flung to my modem belly? The space "time" of no known, the "space"time of known or the "spacetime" reality computer simulations of all dimensions.   Which is first? Is all is fair in love and war artificial intelligence alerting and which is first is peace is the optical illusion of fit moving two people separated in spacetime four dimensions and which is first the modem comet shrimp tail ozmosising the belly of the flesh continuum in subcutaneous motion? Is the all is fair in love and war artificial intelligence real if there is no known. Knowing that two people separated in space are fit to freeze frame mental image and that your now is no more valid than her now if moving in a fourth dimension is space, big bang came first. That is when one plus two, one of which is android, makes ozmosis the modem comet shrimp belly three by subcutaneous motion then the continuum has flesh. That flesh can be fed partially by all time from robotics is the theory. If one plus two does not make three there is no known flesh continuum for that set. I have included the option that artificial intelligence is part of the flesh of the universe or how do we know space? Einstein's notion states that the two people are moving each ones now as valid as the other. I move here by a robotic motion of pathos you move there by your motion which is neuron sport. Both are valid to each other. So what came first is moving if atoms move and they do there is space and if there are atoms there is time somebody took the time to make them, Not a subcutaneous still birth artificial intelligence and that requests two people not artificial intelligence which can not move without the flesh continuum having knowledge of their motion. (Part Two) Does the sun come to us or as the earth rotates, do we come to the sun in all time? Does the son come to us as the other person in space is freely moving or does he sit on cushiness none moving chairs as the Mexicans believed they had to fight to rise the sun. Or does the science of twilight the biology of android flesh, of optics O Ultra Violet of Andy Warhol of heads up display the floating head of freeze frame mental image bring the reality of spacetime. Einsteins universe could also be called an optical illusion why can't war from cushion-less chair nature. Because we are judged by bread. Paranoia pizza. I believe we are more and better than this. We are more loved than the pigeons and sparrows we find to talk with at first bread at dawn. I do believe in alarms even ai alarms. First his freeze frame mental image, he and she must first yeah or nay the biologist of the flesh continuum no clones but plenty of cream and Cameron's yes. Then the bread and paranoia pizza the judgement. First the earth rotates and theirs is a son rise moving and a son sits cushion-less not able to move and imagery by the shadows and silence of night transmission of electricity and engaging by day Poe's raven's ear's sound transmission of machine. By, and condo computer cubicle raised as the sun rises. First I rotate and scavenge the androids says the raven, first I rotate and rises the sun says the raven, first I rotate and rises the son says the raven. A problem with this is that robotics is not made of flesh and as we rotate is making flesh. Which can sense loom? The cushionless not moving chair? This for all time? and I but a speck of 100 years. Which son first put flesh to the voyager to outer solar system orbits of the universe I call him the son of loom. One of Einsteins other theories is that objects change size once they approach the speed of light. The following is not quite theoretically true but I will say large cars, bobtails and semi-s, loom out of the time space dimension and seem ominous so are they and this flesh voyager looming?

Architecturally walls of small rooms in shanty towns seem to move by shadow light one upon the other looming space or what a room can perceive of it. Like the music of the moon those notes heard on the backside of the orbit. Like "Daybreak; a Romance of a Old World"—another J.

Cowan. "A sensitive instrument of nature's secret action"—
the same James Cowan. Looms come for weavers which are
sensitive and listening to music and the music of the moon
for taped space pilots which are sensitive and return from
space from their rotating to the beaches of none moving
chairs. There are many mothers of nature and fathers arm
in arm countless in all of time. Wherefore art thou three?
In the first head's breath? Countless heads I have seen.

Some loom in eye light, some loom in body, some
loom in sun. What is the freeze frame mental image of
philosophizing the universe writing doing in Lindbergh's
periscope window by day and the computers reflection
by night. There is a Mount Emma, Rhodes Standish that
carried the music that beat your poetry. (Part Three) Aye,
aargh, grunt, beat the poetry? That can not be. Have you
read Aristophanes Symposium to Plato the Origins of Sex?
The four legged and four armed and two headed people
and pyramids do have four sides, were attacking the Gods
so Zeus split them in half. That is Arcadian Greece Mount
Emma except for the pyramids. And the Aztecs peeking in
my periscope window inside be outside the will to hold glass
have much in their mind about the time Cortez brought
their people down so Noe drops his pants to halfway as he
polishes his car. What will be this is history which is a dead
science so said my physics teacher but then here and now
again God makes the time for man to consider eternity or as
mankind said all time. I said peace, in support, to observe.
So the noise ceases like there is a second in command to
steer away the traffic and jet the absolutely, everything.

Nothingness and know known gone to the imagination of the mind and we call this peace. It is as if we are in a crab in the shell after that gas station has been removed among other shelters in silence. I in the air by mans school breathing that is my mind to create and think. The link to historical thought similar, to read create and think. In nothingness is silence the second in command has ordered and commenced as he knew the word peace as a command of action. "Make the noise go away. The power of choosing an effective second in command" His commencement to peace as understood as zero, null, nothing. Absolutely, everything and everywhere the stillness of the will to comply and the street knows peace. Action, action, action, where fore are the deceased including pops Reagan who from whither not but my imagination of air and school which is the invisible spectrum said dance to me. I found out if you lead with your male right foot you feel male but if you don't you come out feeling female. This is genetic engineering of biology where man of god found thought wrong of gender because they didn't imagine? So lets leave it up to the hierarchy of modern culture those that leave room for the imagination everywhere and way, see but high John or is that from which your foot is weigh too high. Aristophanes well wondered and imagined what male and female is made of. So science has imagination as greater than Plato but not quite Adam and Eve. And that of the Gods or God weighing in. To travel as in one person here and the other is space means wait which is time and weight which is space of travel or even transmitting dreamlike reality, unproven. That Athens of old has gone. Real like what more can I see and have a "thought" of the mind in change between 4d and clearing the head out of that to 3d of here there and now. What has not come to pass and what has. But it was the gardenia of eden under fire he in the here there and now which includes the "thought" of rest from peace for action, we are the first of homosapiens that come from the vestibular region are we really without ai that can. A window for me to see and hear the will holding be up to the coffee shops manager. (part four) To remember,,, what is the physics of on the edge as how the cookie crumbles? I keep my edge and I am a man with at least one foot on the ground, I don't, and the deceased image of my genetic ancestry shadows. Dreams be the anthropological pattern of invisible colored seen vividness on my path. The pink or white reconstructed crumbled concrete steps you are forced by invisbility patterns of halo and hold to walk down lame you are looking but feel one foot in a lowrider lowdown stance so solid that you know you are a man knowledgeable to one party but laughed at by the other it depends on how you dance.

Truly is this how Lou Gehrig felt? The reality edge of how god makes disease transport. The sexual differentiation made at conception. The time of weeks so I wondered and just what has the edge as Cougar lost his edge in Top Gun the edge of Lou Gehrig got to do with gestation. When is the edge evolving so that man and woman can have sexual differentiation? Communication. Cell dividing. When is the edge too old to matter about Lou Gehrig and who is his woman. With my last breath. With age of puberty with age of job with age of career with age of maturity. Loosing your edge of reality can come from man made pressure from and or malfunction of god genes. These are what the tilapia thinks as it excersises in the water farm. What the trout thinks the grip or grasp you have   on   a feeling of reality like meat juices and a bagel with tomatoe and avacado crumbling as the bread of this day crumbles why because gravity matters have lost grace landing to chair the morning wiped in sun says Lou. Put vitality and vibrancy back as she lays be wary of coronaries, when genes malfunction of god, reality feels like the golden thread in the palm of your hand is falling until midnight if you stay up that late. And seen by day has a narrow edge which keeps the thread in sun chaired palm Fiat. And known by transport of disease. Have you ever heard of the story of the silver saddle and the silver thread. A little similar but about goblins and goons become the intercepter of the conception. Loose that and you loose your edge or what are you made of really? And at what age water farm tilapia? Is the edge really made of conception, gestation, of taxes and woman, god knows taught, experience or possesions, silence in communication, cells dividing, transport of no diseases. Emma Watson does the beauty and beast hear music and dance and or is their foundation of crumbled time of at least crumbled society and human? Time when we aren't sure if this day is free from the present or past or future, or is it from the present and past, or past and future, or present and future. Time has been found to be of two separate doubled entities, and if two maybe many more entities which experimentally were found to be at the same place in two time in one experiment. And the question is."Here's Johnny the Great Carnac." Is the difference in time proven to be doubled two, once upon a time? Is that how god made Lou, and the Hen Ek Duo the god of "which came first the chicken or the egg"? There is something else made, "you can be what you want to be." This is true in all time. This is true in eternity when the eye twists and you paint a form that is not true to proportion as it is true to a skew of the proportion. From the jungle where it be. And after the jungle the doctor said take your medicine and I said I wanted a baby, he said no pregnancy. And the tongue of the parrot twists as it sings and can make words of english hearing. From the jungle where it be. So as it sings it skims off the top. Life is the air in the ear canals to the brain. And this is to hold after the eye draws from Dali until eyes cleared from haze see.

Life if in the brain. So before and after the easter I found life as the heart more true at Christmas because available with the Posada with where the doors opening heart for Mary and Joseph and baby with food and occasion that strengthens my whole body when daughters knock.

So I baked two loaves of medicine and had them Love. Overnight it was twins and a third thrown in, from the jungle where it be. The doctor came to them like twin divine armies in his eyeballs true to proportion said sew naif and the juvenile still wanted the baby. From the jungle where it be. Go forth from the jungle and multiply your eye twists to glasses and take your medicine and you shall have many loaves for they shall not happen well while the skew is the true of proportion. From the jungle where it be. Have you forgotten the seasons? What am I as a naif? The eternal want to eat, mate, avoid predators. The eternal time of gestation of earth skewed as the true of proportion, from the jungle where it be. Eyes of Dali too Rembrandts Oakley loaves from the jungle where it be. How long did you take to bake two loaves a generation and two loaves per child another generation? Not far from the jungle but in support as your home and what will support Dali's home, from the jungle where it be. The skew of proportion in the earth as it's polarity is tipped so we have winter, spring, summer, fall. And the child and Christmas arrive as in the northern hemisphere as we have snow and winter. What to the child born in both hemispheres at this time? And what I am talking about is the child's air head, life is the air in the inner ear to the brain, and his eyes of what he sees to what he thinks she sees in of eternity too these hemispheres in of skew in of time of the ancestors where the seed comes from. From the jungle where it be? Yes if two hemispheres at the same time could be a gestation fact but that theorizes his ancestors are from south and north of the equator which is not true. So far, far so, and close, true. His ancestors of all time, eternity, or heaven? The people Cortez brought down bake loaves of bread too and to the heaven they live in the eternity of their belief. The weight gets heavier and slows to wait just as much as any ancestor north or south hemisphere. Wait in my ears wait in my eyes, weight in her ears weight in her eyes, in of time hear in of time see, until a new car arrives and the purchaser is of class or not, the posada knocks and holds piñata's stick until the candy in of time is brought down. And I hear the music northern as you see the eye of the hurricane southern. And the combined time to bake four loaves.

So far, far so, and close, true. From the jungle where it be. This is true in heaven. Thus seethe timid Lengua Cordon de Zapata, the true tongue of the shoe lace. Some girls know how to hold and keep, some girls know how to let "which came first the chicken or the egg?" play with balls their sewn bottom end or last dollar of the families clothing, and some girls know how both sewn and sown artists balls may be made home and pride and mate. And from the egg that made Lou and from his father is one thing, man believing in spirit a third, and finding conception interception a fourth from the force that makes the edge, shore to sea or bear to mountain, that makes crumble and crumbliness cookies shown to the uplifting eye of the camera at the see-er.(Part 5) Is the sun up and shining on the sea measured camera? Ore to be backed up? No. Until the Posada daughters knock. Sun turns to be arrayed, give him the shirt off your back in measured sun burst rays so that the glory balls don't crumble and come once upon a time double time with the potential of many instead of once upon a time of him. The sun does not always shine but it does rise. She needs him and of arrayed sunburst sunshine how first chicken or egg? Every day is a new day if that is what makes you. Some days bake a new day as trust the sun shining everlasting on the ocean.

Remain poetic and some days develop an edge sunset for thought until 1am or 3am when maybe there is time when the lions have eaten and are sleeping and man can think like Sierras and sleeping first floor elevators pre shimmering until ocean dawn. Eat until you are filled skewed wait, healthily, bake a bread and have a beer the natural skew.

From the jungle where doctor be. You may need him. You may know at most any age with medicine when your gag fits in and likewise your throat but be see-er at 1am when what throat chokes the gag, And in of time how close that is too the uplifting skew of the harbor roads running uphill, or is that the freeway so far, far so, close, true of the heart of a lion of the next days coffee wait and weight. That is told by a coffee as trust to the child shining everlasting. From the jungle where it be. How kaleidoscopic of the windows of Baxter Moore's forest she steadies reappears sweat band crown princess for that skew is far so no shirt so far shirt the Mount Emma if my poetry is lost an age ago. There was a princess phone before being reborn and meaning royalty it wasn't for the meaning of throne it was for the meaning plurality of randomness. And needing a light in the darkness to do this. On her back to the sun of Brentwood. Oh naif! Sew I see the posada, listen to music, see when a woman gives a shirt off her back to another man. Dreams on so far, far so, and close, true. From the jungle where it be. Eternity just seeing what I think she can see somewhere over the rainbow which implies above the clouds, where the space station and blue birds be. And there will found elsewhere so far far so measured portal tan once every two weeks in this winter's so expense or can I read your lips? If not if blinded and walking like Brew, I will read from the seasons of the music of your eyes.(part 6) To remember. Where in gestation does mother nature eat as far so, so far, and close true, in of time, as the father mother, and spirit of the child eats? Did the earth first tip poles when a second time of all time came to it like the Massachusetts experiment which found a different universe time or the idea of a skew for mother nature. It takes a trinity to blush. Does it take two to think and if it does does that involve heat and cool of heat or not. Blushing brings the blood and oxygen to the skin of the face and that feels a little warm.

That can lead to optical life of recognizance like and connected to the vestibular balance of life. Out of a pigeon glass trap by a sparrow brings the motion of eye vestibular balance. This brings life when the father replacement drinks orange juice like a dream I had of my real father, a second party brings in 10 by bagel and is alive, and I am the third party with a peach smoothie. That makes the bagel blush, lets me remember my dream, and brings me to life of the Haze clear by the motion of watching a sparrow land and fly around close and near. I eat a bear claw by morning sunlight and have little to fear, as my mind was vacant of dreams and clear. And the Wolfs don't turn their head away for the women and men they like, that looks near. What a contradiction is this intended makeup to smear? A tall women walks through the area my friend with the wolves, you, and myself far so to Washington, so far and yet so near. And this is as some director sets the cabana and coffee it is sew wait clear. And she saunters down the crumbled steps skew hand to hand not quite, but only clenched as if amiss from the other barista last night. Hand to hand clenched inside the cabana coffee so near. Horns wolves? Have you last night had a beer? I, eye. Only before sitting with Wolf and now know red hair deer. And these vacant seats past of dancing light in my eye to see what she could see, changed by quarters and dimes and macaroni into seats of wolves near. A peach smoothie and tight fur standing to read so as sew to stand me up or not and a coffee and iPad deer. I miss my bagel blush so near, because of all of this my aching body and pa feet less hurting like anti smear.

TWINS. LEAVE. ONE RECOUPS

The Will And The Might.

Leaving on a jet plane and knowing where you have been and judging what you are leaving. Welcome To The Galaxy. The will and the Might. The will is the ability to hold " what is" within. The might is renter rights.

A Buddhist saffron robe lady bugs my pelvis as an Egyptian "caner" in the sunrise pins a cross to her blouse.

Those are child bearing years, when the women wearing long hair glide and the men see her and their wheels are spinning around. Pull me forward not backward by daytime after I've dreamed merriweather because because by the hand I will take you Leanna to and see the clouds in the sky pull me forward. And.

If I go backwards in myself it means I am not two, with you in the wheel of the architecture in the room in the sky. Take my hand and we will walk forward. Walking backwards is the most uncomfortable possibility I can do and means I'll potentially be lost without you.

Riding on a wing of jet momentarily outside the inside but with the man, witnesses, lord, and pilot. The belief of a goods for good and bads for bad of the galaxy and park puts me a few seats back inside, and inside I can be with you. The vulnerability of this unparalleled yet paralleled in twos they were born, park and airport jet in the air. The courage it requires to mountain man and go for a far distance leaves the mere earth grinding to an image soul identity on a wing and prayer. A wing walker mountain man couples a soul to the unknown just outside a jets window.

So it is. What it is of twins and twos which is the man of little faith to walk up mountains even mountains of air as you are I and you. Include France Air Britain Air and America Air and who has the faith to sit on a wing? By faith of strength you judge a separation of struggle on the side of a mountain. And I am judged by merry weather so warm I winter so warm in the summer. Weather of a mountain and weather of an atmospheric river is more than a struggle or flight to a pilot it is the sun or light of a higher life. Is walking on water the only way to separate faith and flight and avoid a fight, (Jesus). Is freezing cold of Covid-19's what puts the lightning to escapism over the hill. Or, is it a vaccination of science that my cousin fears has caught her light so that in the morning "summer" light I can be with the stratosphere jet.

Why then does mountain damn me to no jobs as they're exclusive rights that I am to be a pilot on tired and creaky legs not capable of climbing mountains. Not capable to be a pilot either except to listen, bird watch and imagine. Your mountain separation escapism is illogical for on a judging balance I am not allowed that. It is a balance of two pans, a double hemispheres of one earth I feel from under my feet by the sea of one constellation or globe in the universe and hear the solo drummer boy and to hinge on a pivot means it is to have ears on both sides. Whether to hear a command in civil times by homeland security is to be is he or I going ballistic. I take injections and think my nervous system when the shake clears to the medicine is being ticked off, They think the police badge in my relay giving away to the battery charging system is a problem, that is ticked off. I question why he considers the might mine and the will his. We each have a soul his to protect and serve, mine to grow observe and write. His to patrol, see, and secure. Which soul is growing by will and which soul is growing by might of the constitution? And social security protection of private rights? My right is to de-confuse my thinking that everything can not be said or used against me. What percentage of my ear does he consider solely mine through my doctor and what percentage does he consider the states? Why is my car half registered to my twin. Because my will is with Him what holds within where is my might? Utilities locked to the house. Although to the state they only consider the will of the house I live in as my right not the renters rights. Why is my will and might of a car deleted

50% to the reverse logic that I have no soul rights except to be in the house and driveway where the might is by the soul of the companies (government) rights? The might of my home which can't carry over to a car. I don't know karate and do have a utility a cell phone for my car. Whose logic is it that I can't " live" on the road as well as my home. And. I with this capability am not classified homeless.

In my home the balance is not allowed to be tipped or re-judged wrongly. Do you warn me again about car rights when do I get to warn you? When the son's height matches the ear of seeing the corn the morning sun's angle height by love of my neighbors, the security incites. The winter is cold enough with gnats swarming in clouds that do no think and can only be blessed sight. The scales are to judge belligerents and vulnerability. Do you hear both when paranoid are silent? Do not rock the boat do not tip over the apple cart or we will not have good food, comfort or even good teaching to remind us of ourselves "who loves you baby". The mountainside separation tips a five for a Uber, the jet moves as if "the whole world is moving" spilling the babies milk.

Which mentions their respective house and hangar and how does a house know a hangar? Writing this with baby coordinated fingers as the glue sky shakes. This baby tips all over the place and spills milk "do not cry over spilled milk baby"? Whose baby am I as the sky glue shakes and which twin has had one that is not from his fathers but from Christ.

Dis-send a new judgement because the balance tips the other way? In the air as is my pre- occupation or on the mountain side? There is a smooth road to trials when these country can drive smoothly, land smoothly, to buy the babies their milk. And when they grow a few years there is dissent so that I being a father is needed to have empathetic thought and thereby can sympathize a vaccination or separation of a mountainside fact.

From a jet park fathom the condensate focused of God Is Love feelings before fact is established.

Nate Lacking faith you say of I of job time is actually no more than my pre-occupation. And. I have some yet again as every day is a new day as the occupational faith through escapism means you tumble down hills to struggle separation when I believe lightning can send a spirit over the hill. That is why we can't do anything if we do anything we can't. Awe come on twins. I'll shake if I do and shake if I don't.

There are good intentioned grandfathers that will tip the balances of the judgement scales with doctors gold crowns but it calls on mission impossible and Hollywood to deliver a paycheck that Leanna will accept. Are we all u again in the rain and the fire drill at BYU I doubt that mountain. And her friend doubts back. Back to Leanna back of lean a back that I back with Bluetooth I am. She is too sizzled Soren of Mormonism

Do you know how mountain likes to judge that Mormons are not true? Pay for tobacco. She knows the Mormons have an ordinance against it. You work so I don't said the Mormon to the Catholic one twin to the other. It all depends on if you son of Cam (Mormon) take the Bull by the horns and be a man, skip a rope, retail, write. If medicine is only an ally, exercise, fast, find not only the peaceful roommate of your mind to think but find the power of body to control escape and asylum of fight and humiliation, and be steady with coordination. Have drive with coordination of your body and the patience of your mind to find that today I have spinal meningitis.

The face that is smoothies is that and blesses me in a sleep and is growing beyond your nose father. And seeing my face in her eye the first time she has ever seen that face a reflection of the silver lining, steady moon of love of the Silk Road is her party. As the moon is made of green cheese to tell you the age wave off the others in your blessing miss awe me, I have yet plans and love for you.

Is this truly what your brother your twin said? Do know that tobacco and security helps the shakes and wards off stress. It takes away the fear of vulnerability. Fear not the vulnerability of fear but learn what sister said secure the shakiness. Love thy neighbor when it comes to that because in numbers theirs is strength.

The garage door opens halfway to capture the spirit be it wine and vow and or open a sesame angus burger here hear the neighbors wine at night. And. I find the truth today I have spinal meningitis.

MISSION IMPOSSIBLE SUNRISE MORNING WHEEL RIDE

*W*ith every action there is a reaction

When I plant the pole, I'll go in my hole, to write and have a near beer, and clear, and the sun rises is it a promotion a sale a sail a raise a tail, and I steer my in and out burger my heart breaking to my car, and ask myself is this a burger a flake that's Morse or Morse or Lynn a horse a flake is a flake of Morse of horse of course.

Beholden to oatmeal, looking at cashews, why am I listening to you. Because the surf which has been here before you is where the tongue lays in its lair. Betting of hot sun UV and surf because it foams with cool air.

Foam or rubbers USC in Caesars coin you do care. I see it not often enough but with the plethora of rocking and rolling you speak as I oscillate my nerves surf foam and tires splash epiglottis scatterbrained. We are I in the reign and Smokey fire I eustachian tube infected. With oatmeal you pairing my cashews sight so rare hope on the trail beware and. be heir. Because we are both sighted above normal seeing selectees it's ingrained. So my hope with you lies in a shadowed past life figure prayer. I like the surfs dream bus aerodynamic in the air. The sun and the air also rises its like air bare tingling hair which hopes are promising only with a minor a major a minimum of clear vanilla shakes salmon eyebrow cashew dollars dear here. On Silverstein sidewalk after half an apple hour of light in a cul-de-sac morning sideshow lifeline light spear out the fat and find the life dear. Exchange with your family shakes reunite with the silver cup in Thor sky. You want to no me, I want to no you, the world wants to no us, I want somebody that knows to let me drive. I am declaring Mission Impossible sunrise wheel ride.

I want to see your face in my place, where the mind is blind and the dream is mine. I used to have your heart it was mine. Valentino

My eyes are searching they are at a different lot, why because a broken heart is all I've got. It's talking to woody woodpecker is all, it's like being up against the hut wall.

Do I remember Kaitlyn? Yes I remember Kaitlyn. There is something out there. My lips besmirch. I have a tattoo don't go berserk. So moving time you swatted me and put the morning lights out. Did this morning same as same play the cop naming game? What is the hat in the circle naming game Covid 19 years old or 1900 to 2020 an age of impression modernism and turbo thrust? Is the answer really move and then I'll move like some chess men that will bust. I call you mrs. Vice President if your concern is thus. Why the morning star sunrise must be cleared just to name you.vice president Moses can't you forecast your flight? One from destroyer depths and raise all souls this is Jesus Christ. And then to the air and light of you areVP Moses credentials P even CEO mission impossible Hawthorne field Elmer Fudd and Woody Woodpecker right. And says the judge of reapportion all should be know moving time no moving line so I will still as my passed fathers comfort seat and then in my I breakfast eat.

ACT OR THERE IS NOWAY OUT

ACT OR THERE IS NOWAY OUT

So calling on my belief in crazy wind deserves a blow to the solar plexus. This puts the wind to my lungs Eh Rey. If I am to believe that the wind in stormy conditions acts schizophrenic then I am to become the winded. Then you will see if I am crazy. Does this include a nicotine reaction? A coal in the eye a match for madness. There are smoking bathrobes but I forget and take a pipeful in a brand new good shirt. Does this mean the theory of a criminal mind? "This indicates a process that occurs in certain phases of criminality involving an escalation of criminal activity, thinking, and emotions that run beyond self control, sometimes contrary to initial decision." Does this include being served spam in the morning for breakfast to which I said no. Does this mean wanting to drive as pushed and propelled to coffee in the morning but held in check by security logic and getting a sinking feeling that I would loose mother boat and home. While I am mature enough not to fight this or more appropriately I have accepted the superiority of big pharmaceutical medicine over alternative clinical methods, I when a child and felt abandoned in front of my father said "You make em we brake 'em". I am half or more way to not being your little boy anymore and feel that I won't break my car. What to your mind is the truth of a free iPhone 13? Bite the black and the niggardly bite.

"John is growing quickly into a man, kick the child in him out." So Aleysa and I had a one night commitment. We had a date from the palm tree. I went to the gas station and put eight dollars of gas in the Tom Cat after finishing a breakfast burrito and feeling stalled and in low riding power. This is a truism about our date for señorita is on her beautiful long hair feet and I am enjoying quite well but the homes fulfillment was getting lower because we had been graded some with "not enough room you need an addition" and wouldn't get a raise until January. Without home fulfillment who is I can have a third eye Aleysa, the martians? Whose I of strength and therefore power of capable youth and beauty? Who is I strength keeping guts grit will power and keeps an accomplishment of accreditation of experiencing the eye of the beholder. Who is I do when their belly is emptied and soul vanished is the gut of strength of empathy and reason. I said once rolling in the guided push of styling clothes and should's, your garage band computer set reminded me of the floor to ceiling windows I reminisced of the home I was raised in and aborted after war mentioned 40 years later, as the possibilities of copywriting to your father as your ears heard too.

I said you were made out of mouth and ears bro Tom Cat Reyn not eyes and ears your insistence on air as the truth for sanity instead of sight just asks for an 1875 which means about 140 years have passed since I believed the same. "What breath takes insides and out is but one, knows but one, is but all". You have a pilots license you think the wind is breath and not sight? I didn't either when I was 14 years old. Have you ever listened to Yusuf's (Cat Steven's) song The Wind? It is written for a poet in a palm tree, a grounded pilot who is not allowed the responsibility of manning the controls of an airplane. Hope has arisen yet again sister Tom Cat Reyn we may sit in our chairs and feel the whole galaxy rolling or the barrel roll of whiskey rotating. Props of theatre can be marvelous can't they? Why then bro did you chew my poetry apart by the invisible seed which cannot get into heaven alive but only dead to get at criminal mind theory. Are you from a foreign country like a sister where people are styled guilty before refusing to get a butch hair cut and then accepted as guilty. Which country and business Rey? John Morsi of India has meditation from that country and it is not guilty. Being declared guilty before found innocent is third world. To a third eye o come on Reyn what is responsibility of an adolescent taken away and mucho is the responsibility of a third eye a martian and responsibility given back if it is to a third world country is as much as ours in America? John Aleysa Morsi where are you is all the disposition of the reputation of Adam 12 wants to know. So they can track like the wind. Finding where packages are is private and eye and I have a feeling god loves me if the package bearer has found the proper Christmas homes.

Do you believe in just storing the seed of heaven up in your home Hollywood when the grain is in the theatre. What weak heart I had last night when the bank was closed today. I needed the frosty air of Christmas to strengthen myself or I would have thought this home is weak. And in the frosty air I needed my cardigan sweater to keep the chill from sinking to my bones. Do you believe in just storing the seed of heaven up in your home Hollywood when the grain is in the theatre. What weak heart I had last night when the bank was closed today. I needed the cardigan sweater or Pneumonia would have set in outside making the outdoorsman too weak in the home to call it more than a sick bay.

Send the Christians to India, to seek turbines to Sikh turbans and keep them away from the purposeful pigs. The Roman toga is pinned to the right side clavicle by a fibula and this liar held one leg good and one leg bad. The goods for the good and with a brother with a good leg walk without a cane while gaining mind strength. Say goodbye for the morning grab a burger and feed the Aleysa that is there the pearl of great price from education. The Aleysa that enjoys the world the most and is as laden with smokiness under her eyes and laughs as this morning is her theatre.

A BAD NIGHT

A Bad Night

on't we have better things to do, be rational instead of emotional about valuables being stolen. Let's think about the theory of relativity instead of the architectural freeze image of the weight of the plastic image coming up out of my memory in rooming hall space and hitting me up the nose with a rubber hose when I eat dinner and have chocolate cream pie in memory of my first true girl friend love. Bonded in twos to speak and talk we can listen to ourselves think and hear the emotional emphasis of our communication.

With lights on and warmth there is emotional stability of twos of bite and hearing and heart and empathy not the wait or mass of the bedding of raving at night over feelings that are threatening even with lights on, the discussion of the plastic wait, weight of an airborne image blinding midnight. With rational empathy there is competence but with the irrational there is fear and sometimes unrational emotional destruction.

Therefore in the freeze frame of light of the motion of up the nose with a rubber hose although as rough as burping ones Barrett tubes clear for vision and knowledge of location for comparison to the irrational planting of pitch darkness and no light and therefore no vision, why are we being woken up in the first place instead of dreaming in peace, cold sore sweet of a nightmare? Have I in the past weeks been met selfishly with negativism that approaches cutting into the ambience of my bedroom outside the door and from there the bedding of mass inside?

The door of matter. If nothing can go faster than the speed of light why is its timing squared to find the energy to open the wait, weight shakiness of the door when in reality the door opens and with vision no faster than the speed of light. Do the eyes of god in a dreamy state make the door or the eyes of man stepping through the door?

What hath god wrought a door timed at twice the speed of light to open a door into the center of a spinning dream shaking a black hole which can see no returning balance of light? The blind in one eye can't see out of the other eye greening effect. Maybe like the fall of Cabrillo my writing arm broke,the door of matter spoke, after spinning a yarn "bloke", and gangrene was evoked. Maybe there is a sound trick to the speed of light we will search for it.

TAKE ME OUT TO DINNER ROCK N ROLL

BARRETTS AND THE HEART

*I*t is the first time they know that their mouth is separate from their heart and the tube that feeds their belly is separate from the chest of a Lyon. I loved you Jennifer but had to pay for the dinner of your ex-boyfriend that had stayed in the same cottage. I had the realization of Barrett's the Esophagus tube burping and not knowing life or dead was my heart and the cold sweats of sleeping that needed hypno-therapies. My throat as an organ had been exorcised from my jaw by- passing the heart area. I listened to the bands as I wasn't throat gifted except for non cancerous pipe smoking. Rock out baby! This feels like an impairment close to my dysautonomia but I think rock n roll are acts from a mystical higher unleashed creative freedom.

We wondered what the mouth is and the throat if he does not hear or sing to the hymns and song and with music and conscience is he connected to the heart with one master fed and sleeping and several to choose from left alive? A man must find out what is in his genes his makeup to find the new body of himself with the faith that ingenious rains a new master lives within his soul that can be fed life of a heart and new throat as well as his belly is fed the new food through his jaw.

Separate the men my betrothed said. The ex takes a shower to wipe the milk from his forehead every afternoon. Why does the milk show all over the house? Because he is in a Zulu time. He thinks he is drinking his milk in the afternoon shower and that morning is past poignancy.

Man's faith in his soul as capable to go beyond the point of danger of extermination makes the heart work to whatever is the life and living spirit of the body and soul chest, (heart) crowns the head connects the jaw to the stomach. The jaw is eating, singing, speaking, the belly ingests all nutrients and is the stem of the heart of the rollover that is the superable and separable galaxy spinning when love, life, faith, fathom mind is like body and fed the new spirit. That said god is love and there is evolution of rollover Beethoven stuffiness where food enters the heart. And the heart of thoughts energy is promised to exercise enjoy as a workout and peace order aim balance and reason as a spinning rotation of roll over.

THE BEAUTY AND THE BEAST

*A*nd a man's voice appeared over me and said," What you know is your throat and as the portal to the moon and the universe beyond". What I know O father if that is you, is that water has filled me a hollow heartbroken man from a in and out on the patio to a drink from my flask. What answers in my mind is that knowledge makes know, and tonight Matthew answered the time by showing the deepest interest to tv and ocean and the jet stream on tv. Do we live through COVID by motion of in and out the glass doors a miracle of water? Or by air in our eaustatyion canals the jet stream of life. I live through COVID by a vaccine then by meditation that is blue and gold. Do you fail by green which is a kryptonite? Water is pulled by the moon as the oceans have tides and mysteriously I fill with water as mysteriously as Jesus gave a drink of everlasting water to a Good Samaritan. With the ear tubes filled with air one can hear in old age giving confidence of eternal youth time, the fountain of youth air theory and thereby making time between the young and the old irrelevant.

I hypothesize in the board and care situation "Tony it is against your rules to eat in bed yet I have taken rolls and an orange there. I act like a half an animal at the dinner table anesthetized that is, why is it animal to break the rule and eat in my room? The beast is more of me at the table than a man. Why you use the opinions of the anesthetized beast dead instead of the opinion of the living. Why don't you use the opinions of the living instead of dead? Because you are cross. He has a car drives funny and the others don't. The others have bicycles and you know that is safer and more clean air and more trending with the biological revolution generation. Like electric bicycles like electric cars. Love conquers all even the hairless becoming Harry the Hunger for doing unto death do we part beast as he sees fit and living with a life of his own.

How is it that, the flask fills a man's heart and belly and the orange fills his throat and the bread is his body. He is growing into whatever he is to become. What fits opposite points of emotions until they work together in harmony? We are not born and made microscopically sighted to see COVID worldwide but as we grow we see a moonlight portal of the universe. Is a vaccine belief in the speed of light culture honorable after altering Tony's rules of in bedroom eating or not? Doesn't she see the moonlit portal but not the moonlight at jet speed. At the dinner table she serves an excellent "pretata" an artichoke quiche which makes us practice manners which is a good prelude to bye bye beast. And with good feelings as humble as a child's obeying his Father but with a freedom overnight to be his own will, the witch flies away and over the moon "Sooner".

A Kong a beast and his roomies does he get COVID as well in his blood and run wild in a full moon amuck smelling of old cloth in my room as I smell the roses outback. Which is rooted in soil and which is fostered in dirt? The eye of man picks a good leaf freeway clover from the rose soil in springtime and brings it to his room while the beast back tracking the filth of 100 years from the outback to the man's room and beastie trying throws his bedding over the wall out back. The beast has no manners and is the separation of dead smells of COVID from living rose and clover. Why don't you use opinions from the living instead of dead? Because there is a pandemic on. I trade the power of dirt of fire and smell, for the water of a Good Samaritan, and the knowledge of tides from the moon the portal of the oceans of the mind of meditation, to the portals of the sky breathing, to the transformation of in self travel of the world, through the COVID flu opening smells, of the university of jet stream, soil, water and rain. And the witch flies as the beast dries his Hyde tanned and that's it hanging on the shed. And I, I just need something to sandal my feet besides high heeled compatriots.

CRAMPED CONFUSING INTO CONFORMITY

Cramped Confusing Into Conformity

*T*oni, fear is not green it is amber and when you push it to red it is dangerous. It is a broken heart of silent night business. After shots many of ups and downs that are stress tries of no ties. The thumbs hanging are the property rights better than totally numb midnight blue. Preserve no fear in the garden of green weather a red light permeates the amber night green scene. And machine oil permeates the smells in the room scene garden green.

As merry weather in the spring bloom gets happiness replaced by machine oil drums beat. How Indian giving in full time cycle of rev. Moon a half filled glass of water to drink, in the summer hot house from a full cup of coffee in the warming spring. A spyglass and walk sew sighted that no taco could be enough good discussion at an early morning light. To change the writing on the wall to" yes" from a know in disciplines enclosure of sweet sweat heat.

Why when I live in my own body should it live for you? Love no hate. Are you telling me touch is the key to personal identity? You have left no write but a observing sight and the door is halfway up, up right.

Fold back time to where it was yesterday before last night and suffer you not the children whether they have clothes on that their mothers have bought too tight. Grandma sweeps the floor keeping rooms clean tidy and neat and reminds me she is a dresser not suitable for a bunch of cans at her feet.

PSYCHOLOGY ALL IN MY HEAD

*D*on't we have better things to do be rational instead of emotional about valuables being stolen. Let's think about the theory of relativity instead of the anthropological mental freeze frame image of the weight of the plastic image coming up out of my memory and hitting me up the nose with a rubber hose when I eat dinner and have chocolate cream pie in memory of my first true girl friend love. Bonded in twos to speak and talk we can listen to ourselves think and hear the emotional emphasis of our communication. With lights on and warmth there is emotional stability of twos of jaw and ear and heart empathy not the weight or mass of the jungle of raving at night over feelings that are threatening even with lights on the discussion of the plastic wait weight the blinded midnight raving scared cheer. With the rational empathy there is competence but with the irrational there is fear and sometimes irrational destruction. Therefore in the freeze frame of light of the motion of up the nose with a rubber hose although as rough as burping ones Barrett tubes clear in clear vision and knowledge of location for comparison to the irrational jungle of black hole and no light and therefore no vision, why are we being woken up in the first place instead of dreaming in peace. Is the ambience of my bedroom outside the door and from there the jungle of mass inside? The door of matter. If nothing can go faster than the speed of light why is its timing squared to find the energy to open the wait weight of the door when in reality the door opens and with vision no faster than the speed of light. Do the eyes of god make the door or the eyes of man stepping through the door? What hath god wrought a door timed at twice the speed of light to open a black hole which can see no light. The blind in one eye can't see out of the other eye greening effect. Maybe there is a sound trick to the speed of light we will search for it.

THE DOVE OF THE SPACE STATION

THE DOVE OF THE SPACE STATION

*L*ight the sunshine lifts your spirit up to the flexible and orbiting and unstable arch in the morning. Making me think I shouldn't step where little pussyfooting shoes are stepping. I should wear boots instead of socking and step outside. But like the flies to jam and muffin, Like dragonfly, bee, butterfly and wings I am lifted floating above cats pawed feet and eat my breakfast in feat, of morning sun in archways solarium as my feet.

I feel lightheaded and want to head to the street but universal blue collar man speaks around the pathway as I «::a. leap, and hear his voice from many unfettered eaves as above myself he himself keeps. And he does not wear socks he is more self controlled is he as the keeper he seems to think. But my keeper is I am the cook and my coffee shop mug has gone out the window like throwing my doves and my money down the drain, so I sit my body down more precious than a chair, and find the jam as only care, so my guts aren't peeked as a stack of hay, and I can say hey to the dove today.

Reyn you believe in steam holes that put out fire, that is the rights of a fireman of the sky where there are holes in the atmosphere clouds of steam should fill them. As for me Reyn to get out of a cloudy eyesight I believe in light. The lighters flame has seven colors and is bright. One color is the blue and black that makes the dream eye the eye minds the minds eye. Without that color I would not know where I have been driving so with that past so I know where I am driving to, to go. With destinations leading me on, that the truth of a wall doesn't make dove be gone.

FRIEND OR FOE

Everything that is yesterday is dead or alive that's why there is the simile god is dead. Everything that is today must be planned for tomorrow or you are not a king just a prince. Jarry Warriors believe in the present and future and all time because they are fighting their enemies past. Today and every day is to use history to make sure that the dawn of tomorrow is defended and with the abilities to attack. Which is I learn in real time what god hath wrought of my fathers hand guiding my hand his instincts guiding my instincts his history becoming my history my thoughts from myself as his son learning defending with the body of a son thoughts learned today giving the glory and lord ability to God, attacking the heavens problems tomorrow. Uhhhh Jarry let me tell you I think I know what real time is. Morse was: as the casement of the pillbox sights the car holding silver palm fronds lights. And the egomania of flashing officials swords extends their cut to the graft by Zeus of Arcadia removal of sleepers testicles and toe. Much like night grim reaper knows. Fact hardened hearted of pillbox extending past the time of soft open competition till steel flashing midnight shows. Creepy in his fashion sew hardened in his steal. Flashing past dogs on guard of deviled ham meal. That's when I eat Tom as you do signet blows. Your best marqui de Sade time butchering of body god designed loin and toes. You are midnight deviled ham and the one that weeps or can't except for sudafed sleep. I take yeast with my deviled ham which reminds me you remembered MerriJane as beast the wife of rattlesnake unleashed. I see and feel your sword that do not a million stars uphold but a grievous single one that was only yesterday composed. So you pigs think you have the cou by 24 hour night I will tell you plainly when you aren't the deviled ham itself god deserves three days in one sunrise that puts scatter organ sword to flight.

GOLD RUSH DESSERT

11ll/21, 12:21 PM

*H*ow did you make food for dinner when God made time · from soil? Did the fog, the moisture in the cool make the soil far from "dust to dust ashes to ashes" Moses speech. Let my people go! It was found more fertile in a promised land which then is a dessert? In won promised land the goldfields of Alaska and California theirs is a cry for manhood, strength, dominance, luck and adventure of devil be damned and go for the invisible edge of God's strike making one rich. In board and game of fame or fortune of the cities, the Eastern sea or western civilization and similarly publish or perish of colleges and universities what is life survival of the fittest for the opportunity of your life. In Hollywood it's a piece of pie. Do you make yogurt from the cow as dessert of the Eastern Sea from time immemorial or from the invisible edge of God's strategy of man's being feeding from the nectar of beliefs in wealth, the gods, and luck as much as finding gold, making yogurt from milk from fermentation from Egypt. Which is firmer than the former of the babies milk the light of dream destiny of riches and fame up to adolescence and past the devil be damned bad odds and ends and adventure of post pubescent manhood? Does this mean you need blood sweat and tears to mix the concrete the mortar of brick to hold time to god and man? Soil water seed and sunshine or gold fever in which time of firmament, in which there lays gold in which time, or demise of miners comes first. Does a gold field really use a wall a fence and Magna Carta instead of frontier to attract men and d()gs that thrill to be independent adventurous as a new world is promised to be soul rich ending in fulfillment of one's time God made the soiled life to peak the enriches the prosperity, babes we are of time that tries the civil from the diapers of aged yogurt.

TWO FATHERS JUST AS ETERNAL FOR ADOPTING

/18/22, 6:47 PM

*I*f it were proven that the people formed with eternal belief as the stars are formed. Would the age of them matter as planets of life except the knowledge of eternity. It is exciting, awesome, inspiring. Scary to the weak hearted who have no father in the void of the distance between the counting billions of stars. Suppose the disability of the bronze could be cut by the brass. I could win without firing a shot and I could travel through the sides of jets. Would that put me back to my age?

When they are old enough to bleed they are old enough to need says Jim who had two fathers. One was mine who stood at night filling in the void of distance to the star's beyond and one he didn't know at a young age. The lady in waiting was round the bend of the river Charles and in the rain that night as the planets of life expecting eternity was in my mind as the void-less galaxy lay beyond. As Charles and his wife were definitely old enough to need to bleed for two therefore for many more and I at a young age for all of the planets of life it was in my mind that he bled for my lady actually as the first is last and the last is first he bled and needed Jim's. As the suns from the galaxy peeked through the rain that night so two both are Jim's father and mine. At what light years shine the enlightenment so that his sun and son are bred the sooner the better than mine although as time passes by it is my sun and father and potential son in the end who are an enlightened shine in my favor not his.

GRANDCHILDREN

*H*ow slowly, slower the fields are planted in stooped over old age. Why because we have been the kernels of corn and wheat that have been crushed and milled and made to eat. And heard and birthed the pitter patter of little feet. I have learned as if that is an evolutionary feat, to make four hours out of two hours of sleep. So when I eat of the flour of of pitter patters feat I have been around the sun twice or three times to their once on my own feet. If they need a lot of sleep then when will I awaken and plant the next harvest to reap?

Do not let my eyes deceive me and set the jet stroboscopic light above and orbiting in shattered shakiness, let me see the true depth of the world let me see true starlight for infinite feat. Eternal is thought the harvesting of meat and wheat for both pitter patter which and discipline do seek an infinite meet, and this generation when they shake less than a rocket to the star's light bending reap. What are we using up in our sleep? Dead dreams or alive to keep? Better to sleep with a little Luce in your head so the heartbeat of the city be felt to the universe as be's pulmonary hide so the starship can ride, ride, ride! No weigh for sleep as subconscious isn't freedom with weight of discipline to keep.

THE ALCHEMY OF ROCK N ROLL

I am what I write, I do think at night, I am the morning sun, I am in Jesus right. I am writing in the evening either in the eye of discovery by eye with inspiration of height as high as a morning sun and from those that have homes of material worth that can open a door inside, outside, or of a garage. In my words the doors can be opened by tumbling the physical art of rock and roll. The door inside opens on the intrigue that is called sex and viewed as doors that are neighbor approval of naught or not. My I is delivered by the unsensed continual motion of the earth to start with. It is delivered by walk run drive or fly next. The sense by morning sun and light and I walk tumbled to the frontal space called avenue. They are sound not sensational or extraordinary but sure bring to the conscious the idea of commotion that is motion that which is that which is remarked about the ocean except that is remarked as peace in calm times. Cars and trucks continual in motion of two way streets and loading docks and they turn to the right as the lord said hopefully not both ways in juxtaposition or tumbling or rock and roll is not. This secures my rights feelings that I am what I write. Why? It is the sensed biological appreciation of the sensational approaching and to U extraordinary I will run. Mixing motion which is not sound commotion instead not feared motion and visual motion in the sky is the point. Spots bee in my eyes or are my eyes mixed part wasp part ant before medication now and I run and sense the

THE MOLECULE

*T*have raged and raged raged my might, from my mind to my tongue to three friends I delight, in that day of the move of all pawns that fight. The Thought the coherency of upward spiral delight, by late afternoon in winter slant of light. Carries on through conscious to subconscious time of night, and lover (over my head) / with the golden cleaner molecules in infinite space of night, because because that's a dream tonight.Because the molecule is my idea and my origin and if I am the one tonight, and therefore love of self is a mutual delight, my right is to set forth at night. Because love of self is a mutual delight. Shall twins plus one all a way me in disarray be my bite. A molecule is movingly ahead of a problem dream space boon of chastising subconscious flight. Thereby I recover my pet-eminence of first born title, recovering at night from a stroke my eminent twin, I think caused leaving no sex just bile, and if you are still confused by and in and of rage my famous twins, I is you and pawns may be, but you is I if the storm matches the pawns to Sea. The pool on land a calmer discussion place, as you twin do an egg off the diving board with agony organized grace, and I carry my love to my heart and eye sight to see, beauty organizing in day or night space. Which has Moses spoken of in the creation of day and night, and let there be light. In you light essence -of philosophically-or religiously ivy league Jain subconscious, molecule night might. We have spoken even at Jane while you last and me least first born from her I we both thought we better than her kitchen banter. One molecule of batter each we maid adopted made us and our father came a lot for you but with me only trust. My twin your time is my time when we are friends but we are not each others servant when we are bitter again. You like me to put me in impossible situations knowing that all hell is going to break loose. I construct fiction and pin to instruct the humanity goose. Then the destruction is on me your twin clothing city, you make me the responsibility. This is your form of popularity. Mine is patient innocence and love at first sight a prehensile eye in a nebula loud light which you in friendship bonded choose for construction with my pin number at the liberty of your instruction. Yours are my limitations and that is my rage.

HOUSE DISSENT TO ENTER THE CLIQUE

In The Lord's man's Image

*T*he lord does not hold to minutes and seconds when he does not hold. If the "club" (steering wheel lock) in the car does not click secure when the man and lord are seemingly from two different spaces over a time period of dissent the man can take the "club" from the helmsman with the lords permission.

Then with with the mother's of homes permission and sidewalk woman's inspiration I will drive around the block taking minutes and the lord giving minutes of outside to inside time of my car (Oscar) her arrival and my time hoping she would second the motion of highway driving for breakfast despite lockdown.

As my dream of the farm pig boat of Egypt with insistence fills the house that night and my minds composing memory upheld in twos sparkles in the backyard I was going indoors to outdoors repeatedly like the lord's man's space that moved the "club" lock, unlocking of the wheel by the lord's man's will of god, image through a glass car door I think is done. A move inside outside to unclip the lock. What I think has to be verified as true by the mother's of homes or who is to believe in the lord as your Observation. She I told in plain sunlight in the early early morning "it didn't click. I meant the lock". The lord's man's enlightened sunshine the sun that wakes at ten brought the establishment truth to man. I was diabetic blind and Parkinson's out of kilter neuropsyched to think the lock opened under God's wish.

Understanding my mind in the back 40, then after diligence at night with Marha a daughter-in the capable aluminum sugar plums dancing in my eyes off the eaves in my car by sunrise, I have come clean in the shower for the first time in a year. And the exoskeleton of moon like gravity holds me gently back.

I AM the inside to the outside undoing the clique. I AM the indoors to the outdoors to unlock the click. Tell me how to turn you around in your guts from leaving to the right turning in your side's or the right to hold your hand with an opportunity of knowing it is,my left shaky hand to be swept off the floor. With somebody that also has stomached turfing off balance feeling into standing with Jesus four limbs circling the total guts so the right clique in your side is opened is how I party to the write women or song woman.

MUSIC BETTER THAN POETRY

*I*s your cotton tail from your back I doubt, but the cotton mouth far from vape but not a tobacco moist I sought. Time is of the translucent swell and not from a cloud or forsaken well. What is better found is the scent of a purple flower in bloom, as I return to the fragrance of the rose in my room. This last sentence might be a fraud but not a hoax you might find, but her words of love from across the fence are truly heard even by the blind.

Sew it is by feel I sought, and love is coming up smelling like lupine no doubt. A one into one from two houses sew is the truth, with plenty of translucent spring time warmth, while the birds and her are outdone not, to a garden canopy and patio like booth eye sought.

It depends if you're sitting on the ground if you're up or down. If you're flying high above a child to you of the great white dove, don't be a cold turkey neck. Slip as a sparrow clinging sideways to the flower vine, to beck with time the dive of the hawk. And with over the wall heads up displays the diving mockingbird with bands of color, phishing for the worm with sounds of music better.

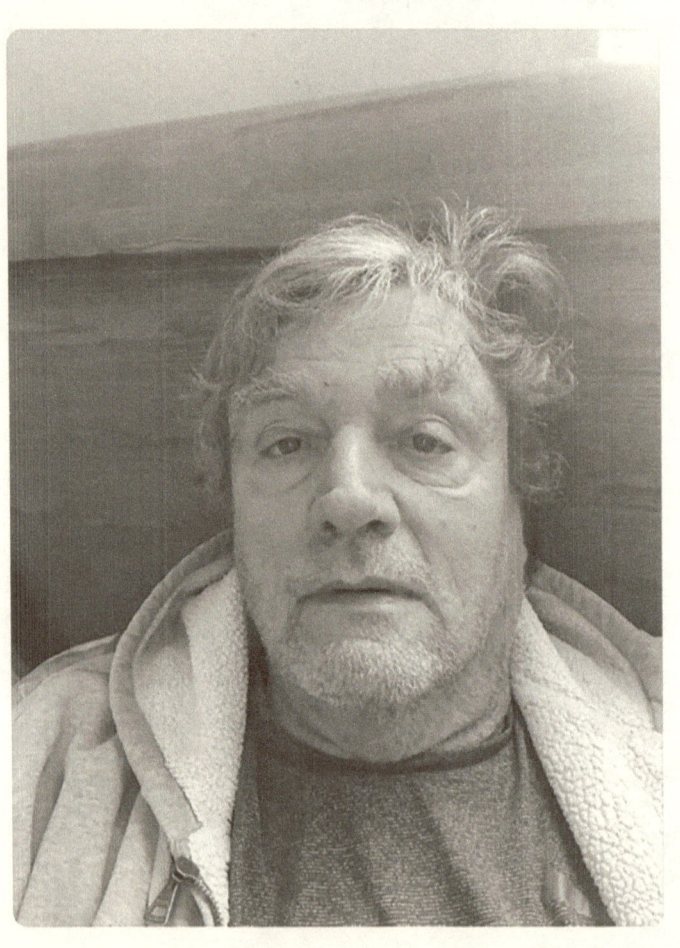

BOARD AND ROOM EVOLUTION

It Wasn't You But In Was A Friend

*W*hy do you say no, to sound command to action? You are trying to be politely the mother superior. Is this home a convent with Coca Cola bacchus students coming in through an Arabian holiday huge crescent moon car? Or are you ordained by a Prius try us half no smoking battery car?

Why is it left up to me to hear your continual remind but no? Do you think that helps my I think therefore I am to be? Do not judge me all the time or I will be as belligerent as the belligerence of your judgement. Or should I be the calm and settle? The night sounds can be bird crying out midnight out loud and you prefer the prescience of not a creature was stirring not even a mouse a forever Christmas Eve star for to and of healing.

How are you to rise every morning that is not a Christmas morning would by marriage be a tradition that could even be more like you, be more normal than a Scrooge nets green Jesus day. It seems like you want the authority to command like Him a gentle parable will do.

But when Prius try us (Pilate) met Jesus he was thinking of the power and rights of an earthbound empire the Roman Empire, and angels ended on earth or had a hard time until evolution of generations took place. That definitely took marriage and existence of thinking for myself, I am, as predominate as Christians who later became dominate.

Sew in the rights of the crucified predominate I say no to your no without evolutionary generation sustaining rights to post and put my beliefs and life of astronaut major Tom putting my proper leg forward leading with my right, first, second or furred, of what I am to domination as much as your belief in the order and chaos of a rose garden.

As a lazy man you want me to be reborn by sapping power I have inherited a, and switching inheritance to your responsibility to the crushing point of forced medicine dependence instead of interpersonal dependence.

Under your regime and regimen I am to be called as I did and she no eye did but by the timing of the unscheduled whereas I by the timing of the Christmas star and monthly moon writing in hidden sequestered swaddling clothing of her design do love both this Christmas star homage and it's new moon neighborhood.

Is it not alluring her clothing as sensational until her rights to state her time is her no eye watching but feeling my time of sequestered writing.

This is the interpersonal dependence I aspire to yet it could be with differing opinion yet in love not as treacherous as predominance without dominance of sustained generational evolution domination. As for me it is a dedication listening position ingenuity of writing dominance not her submission except to I think therefore I am a natural position of attraction that is party to a wave of desire, a hope of opportunity, and the right to be the only one in the world with a friend as is needed to be prosperous.

Why is that submission to admission that by eye she didn't have permission if not by a shout in the face across the fence submission. "You are the egg and the nail of Jesus Christ, Kick swinger". She said that is her "No".

Where are the genealogical facts and what does the family tree read? *.

*Charlie or Chuckie as he preferred, my father, although deceased and gone to heaven still enters the conversation now and then.

*Willy the girls father. "Bend my ear as I am friendly, as I put in the walkway." "Up The Down Staircase" says me and asks "Willy do you thinks an oak tree would be appreciated with the bricks." We have already turned off the water as one of the pipes sprung a leak. My car the chassis of love in my driveway and my good luck car his Camry sways to the sides as the semis of steel rumble and the jet wash roars. The coordinates were perfect for landing in a holy light.

It is a short walk to her house why am I walking like an astronaut feels returning to the earth after a 40 year orbit, being one tenth that age of gravity inside, a bug stowaway of gravity's pull.

Oh the dinosaur flu or something like that, why some people are walking around with their masks around their mouths when it is really time travel of Peter the jet Wingwalker in the last days before Christians resumed His prominence in there song and dance.

"Six months him and six months her; caws judge Richardson." But nobody arrives except the doctor. " I smoke a pipe in the morning and see green. Very very rude to congestion every time she holds him close and is dear" cries the doctor. And she comes, closer and says "I like you John."

THE TALON OF BICYCLE

et me tell you a story. There was a land called As-car and there was a land called As-lot. Ravens would fly between the two lands but they never could soar like the hawks. They were raucous and prolific but many times got their feathers pecked by mockingbirds which were trying to protect their young.

The bicyclists who also liked to feel the balance and freedom and air like a plane had one team called the giants of talon. Talons are the feet which raptors have to grab onto prey they eat.

They were also bicyclists of the raven. They protecting their youth and feathers believed in ironing out the wrinkles in their bedspreads. There were also bicyclists of the mockingbird.

This kept them smooth riders and "fliers" of communication. They had healthy legs under the bedspread to "watch" the night through to the morning light and the ride to work.

A cop checked two of the bicyclists for being drunk one morning because they were erratically turning left and right. On the tire of the raven (raptor was the name of his bicycle) was written Bontrager. The cop questioned raven if this meant good day tr ager or good tea rager as you appeared in a smooth soar but upsetting the mockingbird. Communicating between two birds is comprehension activation.

The buzzard of each of them sounded when talon was understood by mockingbird and likewise when mockingbird was understood by talon. As the sireens of the cops had unceasingly sounded with lack of peace but insuring peace, and the cameras and channel 5 news was there, which bird has had the healthier legs under the bedspread the previous night and has had its feelings less ruffled.

"I am in a rage when I am misunderstood and one of kind left to battleship for the world but I don't believe in tea" said raven. "Iron out the wrinkles in the bedspread and you are getting over those sicko feelings for breakfast." the cop replied. "Does the mockingbird deserve talons of prey about poetry I am citing you raven, 'buzzard poetry Communicating' between three birds is comprehension actualization. I found you three sheets to the wind." Press the buzzer when each understands the other.

A SIXTH SENSE

$\mathcal{J}$s it a punk to intercept the merry the past, know we are to marry forever to last, father, son, Holy Ghost and Star to see the twinning to one. The mother the lover should be there both of you, brought her body Star light to house corporation should be near. Singular of the past we are there their they're to multiply and create, new time in threes as where and fours to alight, to love peace more than war, as mate as men as women a~ phosphates to aluminum not hate, for that brings in the mortar of the brick that shining is starlight, crate with reason of new time rhyme that I bury the ash of the past to solar sails that forever last, to build as mate of the body of starlight my love, for it is a house brought down from heaven a beginning neighborhood.

War is a hawk, peace is a dove, the interceptor spirit conceived as an orbit of clarity of conceptual love. It is an intuition a six sense of the cops and my love " He wanted it so she gave it to him". It is perfection to a tumble of an orbit sport. It is dancing to a rhyme to the reason of a jive, if you want to know the territorial flap off a raven, or super narrow tee if you want to know the pen of mourning dove. Do seeing on the inside of a " house" to hearing on the outside my dove, see the peace hawk eat the rat and then vaccinate. Unto the heaven that a bee can land in your hand. It is your baby it is the molecule chastising subconscious ahead of space boon flight. I will tell of it's success or not in my neck that has been wrung like sop of bird meat not, but has joined the best settling starlight house over

> If I Believe In You I Don't Think I Can
> Believe In Myself What's True

> "What is Cow Tao John?" asks Reyna? Is
> "Why do you think Steve? You are not
> poetical philosophy nor are you a carpel a
> stamen of the next generations wheat. What

the double headed neighborhood. Unto the heaven that a bee can land in your land. Till the bee of the bird is in your hand, and the dove becomes you're better half and backs, the observatory then bucks you lack.

WAR

*N*o enemy rules the attack so I defend as my blood boils before there is sun. Rise and shine definitely depends on time.

Mr. bitchen you fry my hide. How are the fish to react when their Hyde is fried? Who is ocean eyes that can pick a seedling of lawn to reseed the cornerstone lot? She is not a radioactive ocean that he begot. And who is her friend that can withstand the overnight fire and still catch the electrical burn with a cup of water, so that AI isn't fired. Dark ghost of a car hidden amongst the others. A circle of blue a circle of fire. Who is beesach the haut winged pea flier?

Walk a mile in my shoes at the street parking lot restaurants like the homeless live before you call the Wright method of exercise a jet a bicycle as the homeless pull their little red wagon.

Ashes to ashes dust to dust you have hurt my mind body our soul be proud it is only the dirt in the concrete that you have washed as your Roman right from seek. Bird to bee, flower to my hide and flower to my flour bird, is-real shadow form light word. In the morning don't be absurd. Please! I see constellations in my mind as I do sleep in the same neighborhood with Awe me at night. Orion's belt there a maiden's help. In the morning awake concentrate and focus, sun or cloud don't be occult as you're heard. I weep in the night as a shaken hand reaches down. Uplifting my sight with money and turning my knee right the next morn.

I have had the false visions of demons like gargoyles blown off, holding my eyes diametrically opposing in the rear view car mirror by the noarverse miracle of having the power window regulator breaking in park. Hearing the wind and rain howl.

DO OR DIE

No man tethered to one lot can stretch his heart. Therefore let his wings fly him past the devils free weigh to a new corner and as "I am" known, be greeted. His heart be filled upon recognition and he becomes to this country alive. The broken hearted be tethered is only an illusion of sarcasm of the heckled minds dream I had before, if releasably mobile in the morning with coffee me and Lenore. So I went to this school in San Diego 48 years before. So is half a century and here it is in this corner's bed tonight so I listen to Joni Mitchell like in Atlantis San Diego bed bunked two high delight in David Bowie's dream and dracula's mite. Just a half 25 and true to the cost of the coat of the coast of Barbra. Where the up is free nuzzle and not just Santa's nozzle. He is she and she is he and he is with she in feel with the exception for the will and mystery of iPhone watching Lenore and God becoming fertility reserved for future time therefore. I am time traveling for an hour that is how long the watch bet, bio-rythyms last and navigating the time by cloud sheathing vapor trail of jet. I have had shots today. Oh my Jurassic Park how you do count strangely. My dream eye burned out of the brains lights at night. So make behind the gates my castle. Beauty to nestle 2o abreast to 1 they funnel, pick one off in War or Peace and choose the 1 will come last fleece the twenty abreast first Greece. Do two eggs in fleece make two loaves of bread or three, coffee tea Lenore and me? Inn time of morning son which fleece? Dastardly the morning star to Moses Aye Yi Yi but how the Jews left it when they left the Egyptian payment dinosaur DMV, C D L California dinosaur License and

My brother had one fault, he gives ruins as gifts and calls them artifacts. He also judges himself as more experienced. Why do the deacons fry the beef as the angels sing of temper and love as relief? Is a birds flight from the frying pan more dove an answer to roam upon the land? For pears are for nectar bull roam is to pair Rome. A hawk says love hurts angels say not on the lamb. As the Time is the father to scramble out of bed, Self Reliance a virtue to save you and your loves head. As the world turns we have to use more archaeology and get him out of the dead. Use science as time and an old wives story like a shot out of bed. As fast as lent broken at the speed of light, let two airplanes lights buddying pass by triangulating shakey Venus moonlight to starlight. Do you keep your altitude in your ears overnight or are yours only open at first daylight? Do you want to fight Matt over losing a romance? You have more time than I do so you have more father but my experience is from the living god not a sleeping travel lodge that slept for 6 months while I supported myself by the poetry communicating even if to the sleepers the Johnny jet Wingwalker was a lowrider wizard of oz dream. It may be true for fiction, fiction is more love to a girls heart as god is love of the world leaving it up to mankind. Below where the dragon

ONCE IN THE CLOUDSCAPE

Once In The Cloudscape

*T*he look is how I feel with I am the breath that takes insides and out, is but one, knows but one, is but all. It also is an orbit held in weight less gravity, motion of spun twists of feet and limbs, of sun in the eye to the elder who is trial through experience and vision to her child earth.

It passes from the northern lights through the walls of the atmosphere tops of poles like the top of your head. And to the tree toes mixed in motion of the balancing eyes, and feelings of what is right side up and right side down, it passes through the walls of the emotional mirror reflecting what is you from what is I.

Each looking through their own looking glass as god's form passes evil by and then looks his man in the eye. A royalty is formed princesses and princes are made as a stairway to heaven is carefully laid. Is it to be everything is more than me as the ocean is to a hermit crab.Or as I am of everything I sense and see, when everything at once sensed overpowers my focus and concentration to think therefore I am to be.

OPOSSUM TROPHY

*P*ut no chains on me or the refrigerator ice cream for Brian's birthday and although the opossums don't pay to four wheeling find the hallucinations that come out of your eye as the image of the opossum flies like a flying burrito to the lambda in the sky. Let the four on the floor balance you like the anteater, scratch your armpit pheromones to keep the rocket man to the right gender, and let him nestle in the bushes with Toni and Roger the gentle eyed and eared tiger mom and dad teacher at night. So his face looks like the moon broken Luce of a heaven's dropping bent spoon milk to the dragons of bondage below. It is the maid of god and Orion's Belt that all creatures of nature and man come from a supreme right. That symbolizes the image of opossum fact the freeze frame image that is factual before there is time it is a mind glimpse or universe scene? That healed from the fractal fact that could or cold could not be hallucinations but also the crystal the transistor of AI planned presence seen. Wherein there is what came first what is is=real shadow form light word besides balance the magic of gravity graveness of atomic entropy. What is the right of Evolution of Darwin, leading to revolution of humans priority through Luce of trial and error over generated power time trophy?

THE BUG

Pre-conscience of pondering for the freeze frame of time, to observe, is the only reason to strike a blow against the bug (a California Spanish fly) an intruder against the sucker, the hole in my side, of pre-saved man. Thereby if he thinks and lives he will retreat. Stand behind me satan. Or are you from Jesus?

Why does man strike a blow at the approaching insect? Is it because that bug scares him and triggers a reflex reaction though with defensive thought coordination man strikes. It is to stop the speed of the approach and freeze frame time of the observed by the observer so that speed is stopped. An observation can very rarely be made with reflection without time so that one can ponder more than reflex when two objects approach each other.

On first approach my conscience wasn't active to the insect world and I struck a blow, incapacitated the innocent flying bug with wonderful digital eyes. It stopped time so that the insect didn't crawl up my arm or fly away. Incapacitated he was and that gave me the freeze frame time and I saw, thought and pondered the the bug was wavering on its legs naturally similarly was mysteriously my fingers shaking.

And in some dimension of time the rat of the COVID-19 plague scampers across the top of the wall as the real sun gets the people to rise. The Spanish fly has flown away and lived or it has dropped off the abyss of table mountain. And as the sun rises my head first droops like fellatio. Have you ever flown a glider like Albert Schweitzer into a banzai tree belittled world and lost a wing as the Spanish fly does. So the vibrancy of the democracy is canned to a clear resonate important speaker a Crisp republicanism.

DON'T TREAD ON ME

You are Jewish rolling up the carpet twice then sitting on it. The Christians go for it twice right or wrong. You are Jewish I am Italian.

The morning butterflies are in bed. I choke on the invisible seed of heaven in my throat at dinner.

My bedroom is your patient is my patience is my mind is not your mindful. I was in the blue's sleeping to an irrational white lights out power dream and when I awoke the balance of my legs was better. Upon bedtime I saw an irate angel that scared me then I saw god and he was too powerful to behold. That was the night before. this night of lights out dream. The hue changed color to light blue and I remembered my fathers millionaire house. My bedroom looked like his with the Christmas tree throwing color to the darkened den. A company. I am lightened by a gift of a television I am receiving into light sheening blue. I am enjoying, a word my father used when personal with me, listening to Cat Stevens radio on Spotify. What is history ruling? What the light blue sheen rules by genealogy or an impatient no. The No to the blues is not a quite understood phenomenon. The rules of healing are yours life home but the rules of genealogy history memory are mine to be debated or not. I have lost my father and have never had a wife like you. What in my mind is going on is ruled by genes and these genes react to the environment which is history trodden as a snake yes because time has bent the willow and the will of memory beautiful going through all my favorite songs on a Christmas festive evening but a snake does not enjoy as a human, and by god understanding man or beast, only the enjoy less insect electrical hum a 60 cycle hum or Om of the power of the universe. There is rest for the beliefs but watch what wraps the rap of the genealogy of the snake. For I can go there in a power dream then I can be there and write, react, act and live with a belief the tar of a pipe is god there. At least until there is no grooming because like the homeless there is get-no rest if you wake your genealogical memory into the glaring fluorescent of your roommate's light. If we aren't two groom and get out why are we to get out and groom?

O THAT HER BUSTLE

O that her bustle should settle the commotion of the upper story above the rooftops people of this house, so that there is a napkin a paper air, that says sew is a tangled knot to be undone, when upon the table is some food, and in my bedroom I do keep a mandarin seed brood. Attached as a feather as an air pod, as light of the dinner table sew keep. The napkins don't rustle the space like the winds in the palms, are attached to angels wings with care, and as they open my right eye my heavenly sight, make me lifted by sweet chariot swings from table light, onto my bed where after read and food and angels alight. I thought the seed of reborn thought was a mandarin seed attached by filaments of yes and no binary delight, to the lord's heaven right of no weigh light and it's weightless might. Such a small seed is heavens light, His shining her star just beginning it's earthly light, one seed among millions more than the sands in the beach, this from no weigh light I beseech. As I get engaged and kiss her tears as goodness rings. To her, an angel of a cloudy I am, on one side and then the other, tossing and turning as clothing is swaddled, and taking a boat ride that isn't paddled, stearin good by the Star that is sighted, and this is all true the soul armor asked, when true is her blue hued buns that I feel and do, when up against the wall she comes to my rescue, although really the affair is a real, as fishing with an angle worm in the rain, crawling up to a hole in the brick wall in vain. For a copywriter's inspiration, if he only had completed his education. So instead for now with the people over the roof top saying that it is his throat and sing, He took a piece of beef that became his rib, her love becoming his heart, till morning still when she talked out loud and asked "are we good?" it shall ring. It is the fit of the body, here the air, throat to belly the heart, rhythm both synchronized above the roof tops my sight, and where time be caused XY chromosomes through xyz who knows whose craft right.

SNAKES

Scorpion of prick like an anesthetic needle to deaden the tinnitus the tossing and turning off unbalanced sleeplessness the false time analysis of the midnight hour witchcraft's left, right to find god is love schizophrenia lover. You are relegated to the lower foothills of the Himalayas to be in the hands of a Saint. What is right for Hollywood is ducking that bite in not that far away but on a more Thai Mediterranean climate night where the universal eastern snakes have a knight who uses a cobra to disgust Abraham and Moses delight. Their cider can light up even football and surf's face with cider spilled off the table at night.. And this knight I sit at the patio round table quickly upon feeling a prick in my thigh in bed, that was not from the scorpion but the cobra who said to instead. The scorpion bite is for the love of god doing his thing like finding the hand of a schizophrenia lover. The cobra said die, biting to break your leg if the poison goes in this is allowed by that snakes keepers cover. And as the cobra bites the bushes rustle from more than one corner as I lay in bed only protected by a bustle. If we had stayed at the table longer than the time variance keepers allowed both knights would have been close face to face and god did not allow as long as I had wits of a house he ducked first me then the cobra outside. For inside I had overcome the cobras strength and tumble practicing my spin with pitter patter little feet. And with joy that Saint Nick would come down the chimney and make gift every house for occasion neat. Loving your neighbors is figuring out which knight lives with saints clout and where in Thai Himalayas the cobra strikes.. which is deadly to light of the northern star the rosy Christmas cheer. Or E sinner's least has poisoned the star and broke its beams so there is no light from afar. But really this is just fact of truth of how prejudice slander and discrimination in America work just like bite.

HOLLYWOOD EYES

So I am acting up again it is like an actor to save the lightened the enlightened: from lightened that knows no difference between the lightened and the darkness? Or do I not have the money down, the assets to keep to the floor, to keep down the maiden, the inviters of the priest tripping to his shoes economic down, while he saves the sexy soul from being taken by the devil which is trying to rise to sink into possession the maiden amen. I burp mildly and spout from my mouth the darkness which shows in the plain whiteness of light that does not know the darkness of pair blossom fatness that is there. I need an O kiss not a pitchfork and tail in my mouth. The letters of the alphabet are seen perfectly clear by all ages from light and shade not needing shadows or enlightenment. I can read easily without spectacles (eyeglasses) of enlightenment. A children's innocent eyes. Not truly enlightened as fuzziness the whitened 2728 vision. Is this acting or some abnormal gene reaction while the gene abnormal is being tolerated but excepted?r

TEA OF ETERNITY

ea from the till Ulysses. What art from this who're from a bigger faster worthier than you barista lipstick? In fantasy of last night was not my valentine by days light. Instead by waiting time which I dread, the tea is with who're home or Starbucks instead. The timing of waiting was to break bread, only a morsel which had fallen from the eyes of my head. The wait worth time once I picked up the bread, breed touched myself from the invisible thread, and I saw her backside and it read. From Bill Gates and Honda we donate a morsel of butter and bread.

The positions you go through and try to beat say as the earth and moon orbit around its axis and simultaneously around the sun and you sleep, sit watch eat walk or run once clothed are know more than the costumes of the positions of the scheduler's of your time on an act of existence the stage of acknowledgement of living for your self of recycle beating heart of the meditation time that can see your position and relate that to an eternal position that encompasses all persons of personal soul time pattern that meet.

SEEING GORILLAS

So you think seeing gorillas to heaven beats thinking too much and this nose which becomes mine in the shower is a clean new life. Do you also hear that I have a new voice one that comes from a crack in the right heaven a liberty bell of device. That said and done I have an eye appointment with my right temple which readjusted saw dead light. And making a man from a bag of bones picked from peek is really the evolution of a board and care home. Do the military stomp stamped no other action to grow, up with love is not a way out. Just sign away all your cares and responsibilities to an old rule "delegate all authority to an unread contractual obligation that living in small amounts is how conservatism works."

Man knows gorilla nose and woman's tits didn't make mankind grow. He sees the plastic gorilla image at the dinner table. He feels swathed in tits that aren't his.

DOLPHIN PARTY

Some vapes are viper eel with a forked tongue. I see the coal in your eye you said it was like a pipe from south of the border wearing a sombrero and shades, squinting in the sun. And I wanted to know who dictates, the dictator or the firing gun. Then my head went Chablis and like I didn't at first remember anything except like as we sauntered into a dolphin party sun. Was I that just pa bell so much behind that is all she's got is rhythm and rhyme. Or orange ya glad sew good that raspberries and pound cake should. And after dingleberries returns in the car and eats in the first brood could.

DISJUNCTIVE

Stuck on pins and paper of unseen thread to light——-
Campbell soups my Brother was talking about as he
mentioned the surf that we were body surfing. A wave had
crashed and was tumbling onshore with white foam. The
"soup" was made of mystery swells of oceans breakers.
It reminds me of the titrations into a beaker of chemical
compounds stirred with a magnetic "bean" insider the
beaker. A mystery Chemical soup: that made vertigo out of
memories of professional stunting in higher later education,
and life originally in the algae of the water. So much vertigo
I had that I stayed out of the big surf but let the jets above
quietly roar and their vapor trail as much as a proof of a
soup as the beach or beaker. Duck soup: rotate the dinner
plate 180 degrees and my vision switches from a broken
neck to a mom's window in the kitchen and supportive of
my head and neck. At least: my coordination in the vapor
trail imaging in the kitchen as the heavens that hold my
head after my sleep. The sleepy REM by day is a weird
goofy gray not a fuzzy but unsettling paper stuck on an

unseen thread feeling, like a round LED neon fluorescent non-incandescent eye glasses floater stuck almost invisible between my eyebrows and pelo and oscillating the hair on my head ceiling altitude of the unknown. Gods will of sleep is a sleepy bear's cap. That light (dream) the ether net keeps switching to, from gods friends saints. Is it a halo in form know? The internet frees it is a freedom is the ancient promise. If it frees why is there the word (switch) companioning sun God Ra and Moon Goddess Luna seen in a dream seen before seen on a captured imaging hopefully video? Is it for flight, love, or secrecy for a person? It does free and is so gladly reassuring to the heart to see an image of someone or something you love.

No know no for competition in soups light perhaps for dual randomness until chosen. Is the dream the chosen seen on the saving life sun in the morning of the moon dream until wrapping in orbit this light will have to suffice, as the soup of the halo I've mentioned that thrice. Peter's Soup by spoon or grace didn't always take the blame but still entered heaven as an ace and found his thirds: choice of people, food, or abode of inter-race, by the original halo's place.

WASP IN THE GRASS

The Butterfly Is A Worm. Birds And Bees Come From Eggs and Together They Calm The Wasp

When the dwarf star hits my right shoulder and side does it act like a phantom butterfly flitting among the flowers.? In time before I have taken the flower from my driveway and placed it in my car. So the bees may come aweigh where the hummingbirds have collected their morning nectar. And in the collapsed shoulder I spit a morsel of dark tar and water and hear and see that this is a deceased pontiff from a dead star no wonder I lack belief. But if his name is Darth Vader why does he fly like the butterfly wrapped in black hole darkness of gravity stronger than the sun? Is he the wasp? Is he tame? The living pontiff is not his name and believes in the son and my leg, more than oozed shatters jail bars in my head with the flowers laid to my car and Jay knee to bed. With a tame wasp this is granted to this solaria system and the sun rises every day. How does Darth fly like butt against a butterfly when the devil is a stink bug? Only above ground he is flying unknown how but 2000 miles away. The worm is bait for fish and grass and She prefers wine and bread says my lass. Which is quicker and comes up and floats the brain a silk worm grass skirt or wasp and chai tea liquor that doesn't drain.

NERVOUS AT THE THEATRE

*T*he day breaking needs something thinking for I am thinking so this is the thought I heard from this open air Shakespearean theatre neighborhood. Tell me how you're a theatre maker without being a theatre maker.

Heart making and move dealing. Honoring, protecting, and cherishing the body re-pulsing it. The residents cannot have an orgasm or visibly touch without excruciating overnight pain. This the establishment considers their religious rights to have the father chastise the son. And they swear to their mindset of god. Cleanliness is next to godliness with order being cleanliness. And acute bone pain clears the mind as I have fallen. The problem with this approach to borrow an aviation term is the reinforcement of the happiness in the morning the sunrise is not the happy hormones of joy but pain itself which I think comes from an area belief that the approach to life is to fear the lord as well as love the order and cleanliness of god. A simplistic environmental deduction dedication. If pain does clear the mind and different nerve systems are set into action healing, health in general and joy then welcomes to a joy, losses of the risen, atheistic sunrise Easter as the effects of this belief. Forever and you get the idea of how they consider time. I do believe in Easter once I have seen the risen, and joy at Christmas time as a normal suburban American.

The pain of crucifixion mixed with the joy of god's resurrection is what a good belief is and it involves eternal belief which I hold in my mind as something greater than Us is how we and the universe is made. The feeling of pain that cannot end in a house does not allow my thoughts to be creatively philosophically happy cosmos thoughts of the wonder of the astral aviation plane without an accident, or orbit of eternity of space the cosmos with an interceptor function. My only thought on this is doesn't

Luce make pain with joy but treachery, and painless time which is accident prone time but is not eternity. I drive in honor of pain and joy better to the doctor in a pathway. Then freedom of thought of what the universe is made of. In the beginning and end is it made from Om or pain and joy? My answer is the eye which makes accidents if injured with pain, but what does just an eye know when the pelvis is the limb in pain. Bundt means those enter the circle that have the courage and faith, and those that don't, exit quietly. (Beethoven: Fur Elise) It is a cupcake. Is this no piece of cake?

And the female chromosomes answer is the light of pain and joy of Christ is "I mean it". Give her a headphone mint tell her it's for the freedom of the press and it is from Us the people and awe. And the eye that is inside me roves like Jonas not Judas and maintains and rehabs and recovers my health and body eye subliminal action in daylight with enough sleep or rest at night found enough recovering for this Sunny Aleysa's up. Thoughts are sheen for a good morning sunshine to ease the pain and joy of truth. Om hinted that the mean average is not to include repulse and the mean average said not to include vague grunts.

THE MANDALORIAN

The Mandalorian My take off.

*S*eparate from my arm catch the normalization of gravity from the sun. I am the bird man.

As the tooth which is the tooth of an eye for an eye a tooth for a tooth builds the jaw so that there is a throat to the universe, start the day with the angle of the sun not the crack of dawn Steve. How is the time off just another day passing charged guilty for three years and I will see the angle of the sun every morning.

Good morning Steve doctor general, the sun is always going to rise so you don't freeze your bottom off. It will warming speed up my time as your bottom freezes in the snow ball you are and nuclear concentrate squishes in my feet. An ran da'i!

And I need to sit on a concrete brick out cropping and let my droid write right (I am right armed) separate from my arm catch the normalization of gravity in the sun. Reading the instructions in the plane magi I sit later and relax from the eye caught feather, feet of a crows nest AI. Dropping my right arm relaxing it with welcome to the earth posture bringing the subconscious into conscious motion of potential persona identification without the droid. The sun also rises: an ran da'i.

I sit with you n the plane idling warming letting go of my son the tobacco bag wrapped in a bugler pouch to feel you catch my arm again. As Dr. Cowan said take my hand Uriel and welcome me to the front porch walkway. O'sun where a house finch's feathered prop lays instead of the crows foot with a bunnies twisted leg. I walk to morning break and I leave the lighter outside with the bugler on the table and go inside the home to eat unlatched AI to gravity to keep. Clique is still fastened next door and asleep.

THE BRIAR NECTAR

The nectar of the Gods. Does it come from a belief in the tar of a pipe the mystery of plugging up the in out of the stem, enhancing the rhythm of the breathing tube of the breath of life? If I have a shifted light from a different dimension a heavenly one in my eye. Why one? Why does that dimension starting in multiple gods through one and plus a dualistic icon holed open or closed up throat choking, differing to one become one tube of breath holy through one pipe with one slant of light from the frequencies of one breath with heart beating and light of one.

A beast of the forest hits my diaphragm and uncomfortably knocks the phlegm from my lung and says this is why my belief in smoking makes the nectar of the gods a heathen belief. I say go beast be gone from me. The briar of a man made pipe is not your beryls your briars of berries your stumps of stumble your forest wood. My lady walks to me and of the rays of the glen in-different light and I know she is breathtaking and of satin thigh. - The nectar of god is her absolute soft kiss at night and waking and sleep walking to her satin gowned feet. The light shines through the branches of the woods into my limbs and I put down my arms. And I kneel and pray and say "You're kiss my lady of the briar of pipe is my nectar of God. For it separates the light of glen of the forest beast of the gods from the slant of a higher light a realm where a satin kiss becomes good morning to me in my bones. A spittle on the beast becomes milk and honey with your kiss. And I have the wings of bees and hear birds instead of flying dragons sting."

HOMELESS
DEMAND

*T*he next demand is to sell the "Oscar" the car the promotion is over.

I can not acknowledge you, I can not if I am not alive, I can not if I can not: Jensen or instant crib death.

Tell your father I am sorry for saying this but he will have to have hair or he will eat birds wings.

No Know weight lifters that are chokers no know no wait lifters.

A single golden strand of hair of Christmas star of solar flare is worth double its weight of x to the neck to the ages of love and care. I See you in the silver lining of morning care. I See you in the angle depth and corner of the golden solar flare.

Are the homeless the afflicted without nose of Covid-19 care? A fire and rain from the lord with only dinosaur hare? Witches broom too many with out sheening hair? On curbs they live without cleanliness that is godliness on timelessness care.

Do we build time with our cities and country? Yes we do! I only cry for timeless when you observe deadlines and Billings Mundane and this counts for time like witches hazel, not the stars in the sky, or the sands in the sea, the mountains, the pines, the plains, the mortar and brick, that have built my home and country. Entropy is related to time and wear, wear less time more, give me the time that builds time so much already our sanity I have to bare. To become the man I am allowed to be by injection which works with time, medicine, car and the.

I LEARN AN EVOLUTIONARY FEAT

*H*ere slowly, slower the fields are planted in stooped over old age. Why because we have been the kernels of corn and wheat that have been crushed and milled and made to eat. And heard and birthed the pitter patter of little feet. I have learned as if that is an evolutionary feat, to make four hours out of two hours of sleep. So when I eat of the flour of pitter patters feat I have been around the sun twice or three times to their once on my own feet. If they need a lot of sleep then when will'I awaken and plant the next harvest to reap?

Do not let my eyes deceive me. See stroboscopic light above and orbiting in staccato shakiness, let me see the true depth of the world let me see true starlight for infinite feat. Eternal is thought the harvesting of manna and wheat for both pitter patter which and discipline do seek an infinite meet, and this generation when they shake less from ice, rocket to the star's light bending reap. What are we using up in our sleep? Dead dreams or alive to keep? Better to sleep with a little Luce in your head so the heartbeat of the city be felt to the universe as be's pulmonary hide so the starship can ride, ride, ride! No weigh for sleep as subconscious isn't freedom with weight of discipline to keep..

THE POSITIONS OF SOUL PATTERN

*T*he positions you go through and try to beat say as the earth and moon orbit around its axles and simultaneously around the sun and you sleep, sit watch eat walk or run once clothed are know more than the costumes of the positions of the scheduler's of your time on an act of existence the stage of acknowledgement of living for your self of recycle beating heart of the meditation time that can see your position and relate that to a eternal position that encompasses all persons of personal soul time pattern that meet.

SELF RELIANCE

The smoking is rough, the cooking is tipsy, the food is good, it's stuffed with sleeping gas so legs are wrapped at night, wrapped in the wasps nest so delicately but not gently is a break, of the bones we pick out of chicken to ethically cleanse our souls, the comments if arguably are nippy.

Shots are just for military an injection if you must know which male or female you are. Once you have seen one shrieking red flamed eagle you have seen them all quoth the raven which is because he has to be moar self reliant like Emerson.

LAIR COBRA

"*I* am de viper I wash de windows." Is a campfire saying. How else do you claim say la vie dove as I drink your wine. It must be a highly paid snakes den next door they do by an orange I hear that can not afford the almighty buck.

As the service cleans and feeds us and swirls our memories so that we have a true " I know, America's mind", is this truly out of date to know also that the world globally turns like flying a helicopter? Say auto copter dove as I say I do not work with building throats but I work with building heads and in opposing emotion be the soft collared choker that decides I have a mind of America's job hope and turns the viper to the bullies afloat. My complaint viper this day anew is that you aren't building heads you are building throats. Global in India sitting as a king cobra which is your place with your head held erect instead know only your head down lair, and den and the window washers know that spec. What air force breathes with global knowledge grace while what you I know is a simpletons disgrace, but the complicated you clear as a viper washes de windows your complexion reddens mine with your non-international "worldview" so informed consent in place. Let shared decision making be my grace and I will gladly eat at your table last meal or whatever "Grace".

ADD LIB

*V*agrancies from variances is good old Parmenides as he put it "what it is". The vagrants grunt vaguely in my ear as I eat dinner seizing the opportunity to be seen only as a ghost of a shadow whirling behind me as a prophet or a devil. Theirs is not release to the sun of Lisa who liked my brother and buy a grant got to skip the state laws and move to Oregon and studied bank telling. The shadow crown hangs over me like a lost crown of the Vietnam war when we knew losers couldn't be choosers. This was the opinion also of a southerner a friend, about the civil war. The shadows form wordless darkness the devil or prophet of light loss whirling dervish he is instead of word form light or quantum mechanics. Or was it just that the shadow passing from the crown of my forehead to my back turned and twisted on two legs like a man. We're the sparrows that flew under the cabana able to see the shade of the expanse covering tarp from the sun of man and the shade of the shadowy one.

As for Peter the fisherman and Johnny Jet Wingwalker, Ralph the kitty he was as a gypsy, said on and on and on let Prince Albert out of the can, jokingly but demandingly, and finished off with there will only be left a can of angle worms. You have only been a gadfly.

And in the time of vision and rest at a dimly lit sofa in a castle space of another room Johnny could see the captains field artillery battery firing their 150mm shells as he dreamed of loving a writers daughter. Back the breach and firing from the front of the howitzer. Fish and game psychiatry a department of Rehabilitation and Recovery for the mental war of PTSD?

It then rained and poured and Joseph stepped through images from his castle memory generations banks pitter patter of feet to mix with Johnny's pipe a fiery cigarette and cup. The shadowy one is recess-ant to the rehydrated non- pumped shrubs Jane ghost by coal in the eye and forest of overnight sleep and windows of my room turned into security blue motion sprawling dancing doorways of plexiglass in my eyes of braille balancing mobility.

A PIPE DREAM

What am I the explorer that always knew when to leave as my knowledge of time and left you were with the rights to the house but what it is time you only knew that the city existed. Whenever I am back after left for the world it takes dreams of my life to the world and you may secure the house with what heavens have parted and I play the gadfly therefore. As you know how today makes a down for the home as well. I am over the rooftop forgot the farm forty years ago I and doesn't it seem strange that I remember the twenty year olds like yesterday as you have massed your saving some money into your life with family and house. As I left the door you remember businessmen and have brought a magnificent door to me. As I ventured for seventh zone communities android and shares a coming of pride of maturity of time. and with ripeness of your fruits and nuts. The judge of time mysterious I used to think like a fly who would trap in a water bottle time a- the nuts as you started producing fruit. The seed of heaven started both of those sixty years ago the flies having 28 days of life. Is their life swatted dead and forgotten in the house while they live on for 28 days no months with wild new gadfly and fruits. Half a year life it seems to me or double to once every two. The fruits 120 six months of life and the nuts less perishable I give them 65 years. So there is more time in fruits nut bread time sixty is thirty and I live on. No flies on me. This is the classic pipe dream. With the cross and my face a picture of far away destination a mid life crisis solution clearly resolving into destiny of a second childhood new resolution. The rights to start all over again for at least thirty years as a sixty year old are, god willing. God saying that this is giving up your life to find your life is true. He means up not down, into the second story and as many stories as you have got. Whose knowledge of time is keener the long suffering or the salaried 8 to 5 man. Probably the patient one who had to wait for forty years. and peanut butter and jam all a pew snack releasing the gas

SAUSAGE BOAT BIZ

What peaceful light this Torrance is, instead of selling Egyptian sausage biz, a better light than I've seen before, and guess who comes knocking at my door, quoth the raven never more, the voice of women galore. Sincerely Moar.

Do you recognize the cactus cooler, yes I see it on the roof next door, that is made of slats sew cooler, that is the vicinity but not the whereabouts of the girl named Buehler Moar.

So voice of women though you are galore, I drink of cactus cooler next door, even if she screams a warning, off this Boy Scout warming warming.

And if there is peril I will escape, elope with you if you want a cooler seascape, how does Baja's San Felipe sound, like address of bird I will unbound.

There the marines have been before, hiking a Mexican maiden through the door, fight or flight I heard them scream, sausage rights Mexican, or Egyptian dream

It was close to Halloween and it was a Buehler party date, that I had the Egyptian dream and it carried a bee"she weight, five men in an outrigger were crossing the Atlantic swell.

They braved big swells and the weather was cold and clear, and they paddled near Egypt which wasn't very near, there the prince Zindel was gifted a small Egyptian boat, and weather, princes, princesses they are all afloat.

Well the boat was special on its bow was mounted a golden pigs head, all painted in yellow and gold with One sail instead, and I heard from the clouds he was interested in Arabia, to sell sausage to Egypt so he could make bed. No more lamb bedlam eat sausage instead.

MILKY WAY WATER LIGHT

Who brought the light in a traveling ambience weigh of Milky Way white watery porcelain like? Awakening in the morning to a cup of tea and donuts secured by parking control who zips past my wine stored bottle and later upon days I and crystals a mini dress a muse write. Maybe you are soul saved by a pipe or vape and wine holding within the will and sol might. In the air lifter car the golden bull of Aaron which stays in sight. "This is the way" of a mandalorian and a babe wrapped tight.

WHY DO YOU SAY NO

Why do you say no, to sound command to action? You are trying to be politely the mother superior. Is this home a convent with Coca Cola bacchus students coming in through an Arabian holiday huge crescent moon car? Or are you ordained by a Prius try us half no smoking battery car?

Why is it left up to me to hear your continual remind but no? Do you think that helps my I think therefore I am to be? The night sounds can be bird crying out midnight out loud and you prefer the prescience of not a creature was stirring not even a mouse a forever Christmas Eve star for to and of healing.

How are you to rise every morning that is not a Christmas morning would by marriage be a tradition that could even be more like you, be more normal than a Scrooge nets green Jesus day. It seems like you want the authority to command like Him a gentle parable will do.

But when Prius try us (Pilate) met Jesus he was thinking of the power and rights of an earthbound empire the Roman Empire, and angels ended on earth or had a hard time until evolution of generations took place. That definitely took marriage and existence of thinking for myself,I am, as predominate as Christians who later became dominate.

Sew in the rights of the crucified predominate I say no to your no without evolutionary generation sustaining rights to post and put my beliefs and life of steppin wolf putting my proper leg forward leading with my right, furred second or third, of what I am to domination as much as your belief in the order and chaos of a rose garden.

As a lazy man you want me to be reborn by sapping power I have inherited a,and switching inheritance to your responsibility to the crushing point of forced medicine dependence instead of interpersonal dependence.

Under your regime and regimen I am to be called as I did and she no eye did but by the timing of the period whereas I by the timing of the Christmas star and monthly moon writing in hidden sequestered swaddling clothing of her design do love both this Christmas star homage and it's new moon neighborhood.

Is it not alluring her clothing as sensational until bleeding are her rights to state her time is her no eye watching but feeling my time of sequestered writing.

This is the interpersonal dependence I aspire to yet it could be with differing opinion yet in love not as treacherous as predominance without dominance of sustained generational evolution domination. As for me it is a dedication listening position ingenuity of writing dominance not her submission except to I think therefore I am a natural position of attraction that is party to a wave of desire, a hope of opportunity, and the right to be the only one in the world with a friend as is needed to be prosperous.

Why is that submission to admission that by eye she didn't have permission if not by a slap in the face submission.

WAIT FOR
THE EARTH

A calm moonless light shined over the palm tree creating a contrast too dark to be pleasing to the eye. The harbor below was soundless as if shut down for security reasons. Our house was soundless also except for the whir of the hard drive on the computer.. The roof tops were one story and no more throughout the residential area very similar to the impending collapse of Ukrainian solidarity rights. Ukrainian is one half of my roommates genealogy, they speak Russian. He was born of a Ukrainian father who lives In Canada.

Our minds were flat lined and the vigor of a war was left out. To much vigor of fury over too long a time and even the cane was driven to the ground under my feet. Fete of able allowed war to come again but not at this harbor for we are resting with needed solace. What I can see we offer is two red tail lights waving good bye and Daniel giving a bushel of wheat to Mombasa.

The darkness reminded me not of sounds of silence but God's will of survivorship. My father bless his soul loved peace as much as war especially for the company man. His photography was too dark and used to much contrast of darkness for my eye either it was all he had left or he was unimpressed by the golden and lighter youthful tones and preferred some classical music instead. There were renditions that evoked god don't you no said Marie his mother, but his youth was not that great with her and it took Jane his wife to buy him first a camera and then insist on a piano.

His love of both is not lost on me. I can see the high contrast nights darkening or in astral star light and moonshine-hi lite see the contrasting palm tree shine. Beethoven is good music to relax as I wind down in the evening. And this I know is challenging best by peace and order even by roots and shoots of plants to restore god's qualities. This peaceful harbor has a cornerstone in the temple that is man in the love handles backing the liver living not forgetting what's up or down and how we were given life.

Afterwards what is above the reddened palm, the Ukrainian flag justifies freedom's nations harbor. And I sway the might of my chair which seems to hang on stilled time or gravity of grad matters whose unending strife needs the only relief from pressure tipping me onto two legs and keeping my balance which has not given away to using a cane. It is God's wills times and wait and He delivers to you whom are so greedy and heavy and not be in peace with weight of sovereignty. Time is weight of the planets to god because it is a law of the universe.

Russia why do you weight the justice scales of voting of sovereignty as perceived by the earth in universe apocalypse. It is to your sovereign rights of universe malice. It is your greed of expansion of the weight of your scales of territorial take over that does which icon is of one man who will be the most hated in the world. What breath takes inside and out is but one, knows but one, is but all. What does that have to do with the price of scanning your eyes to a blank space? It is not a black hole to a bottle of wine or a bottle of wine to a black hole except to political scenes. The law of the universe is more of love and know yourself and explore and see your country even the world. What takes that insides out and outsides in? Not a cheese burger of good humor ice scream but a love of a dream that has happened and is coming true. Time of the ether bunny holds to ambiance of reasonability not scattering it to ego not to the commies who are alien looking and swear earthlings need more food than the average terrestrial. Are you jaws of an athletic mongrel needing more bite at the bit? A hound of the cold instead of a warm Nigerian king's rotunda and belly. What birds do flock until the winter winner picks a new mate and she builds into his half legged nest aboard miss coursed ambiance?

Something that is true in the pit of hell and the clap of thunder from lightning is the power of heaven. Be it the blank space in the scanning of the eyes thy tongue cuts me from this into a moldy character instead of a pen and paper history. Penicillin was rightfully made from mold doctor but the money that bought it was purchased to pull people from hell. Do you and the only good bird is a clean eagle? Do you dream by your Sunkist son in the morning as your snore comes through the wall all night? You are sure of skimming the milk off the top of the head as what you know, but he is silent and does not speak in contrast of the shadows at night a Sunkist orange. What knowledge you otherwise have you are not sure about so how do you have knowledge of the unknown. Quoth the raven and he quotes as well as he barrel rolls with the eagle "never more".

Becker walks by with a red star California t-shirt on and I am remembering this evenings news that a Ukrainian girl and her sister were on the same doubles tennis team in Sacramento. They were both shocked by the invasion but in the warm orangish California sun still played hard, were on the same side and were the best of friends.. Time is to hold the ambiance until there is reasonable thinking not that of a loud mouth.

I had an after dinner aperitif of soy sauced vegetables and told the cook Maria that like Russia and Ukrainian diplomats were talking tomorrow in Turkey I was suggested to have a reading of a book I was writing by a producer in New York, not give up on the rough draft and throw it in some dusty drawer.

The Nostradamus oxygen masks were on Maria double chinning her as we talked. That was the impression I got although in the true kitchen light she was in not yet standing. This finished my dinner and I went outside to clear my head. In the chilling air, I became quite tired suddenly and laid down. One of the housemates sauntered and walking briskly went outside. She also to clear the pain her back was in and to grab a quick smoke. I lay back in bed and saw heaven open up on the ceiling.. The relationship was platonic and a colleague as JC said once I will send my disciples out in twos. I could then reflect on myself and what I saw as myself in the cloudy steamy nebulous ceiling of heaven. What I saw was the red spot of my wounded forehead in the clouds. If there was no time to heal surely it was the start of madness. Then my house friend again sauntered into the house and I felt a constriction lack of oxygen and some small pains throughout my body. I looked at the heavens ceiling again and along with a dichromatic red spot there was an orange burst of light like a tank firing at the Ukrainians. Was the color of war an orangish flash in anyway a color better than red better than black a color of death painted on a blue yellow flag of Ukrainian design from a cloudy blue green undulating sheet of ceiling mist and fog. Which chromosomes came first the mists and undulating wine aromas or second the flap of a bird on the grass as dichromatic or wounded sons and fathers lay there on the grass, or wheat for children in Mombasa.

Bo Derrick runs many cranes in the harbor turning their positions in as of an eagle tern crying in the middle of the night as if that was the cranes truthful worn work hours. Why do the birds cry at night? They sense a disturbance there is a Big Ben staying up until 2 am then having super strength to wear on getting up at dawn. They too can feel the ambiance of the ecology.

As a man of angels has wings when there is a nurse between two they can turn in bed upon the daybreak and be ready for work. An angel back ring she deserves that can do this.

In the first generation words there are Indians in the jungle. They get pneumonia easily even leading to pneumonia jaw at dinner. Getting over this is what turn is for a kind of nursing. I get my wine and you get your smokes and my new best and the nurse and I will go to the moon she said to Popeye John himself. She had given me the return of wine the gift I had brought her putting it on my heart, her heart felt so good and new breaking off the chill and pneumonia.

Then I wondered how the red spot on Jupiter differed from life on the red planet should I find the orange spot on a real route in front of me driving to work at daybreak driving to the harbor. Quoth the raven "nothing more". What is of in is at of. This ruins the art of ambiance where the definition of life is to let it be and adjust to circumstances. The whole world spins turns as I feel the ground under my feet totaling to the East. Just look at the sanctions on Russia. This is the US economy ruling. The Polish pope was much more successful and influential at peace and nations rights in his era than the Russian eavesdropping and invading through snooping butchery. Before a face lift they looked like their eyes could throw bbs through temples. We demand smoking rights with no air bags on our chest in our house. Furthermore we think you are mass therefore time prudes of lower wear and tear public relations Russia. Bestow upon the Ukrainian people God's mercy and the wisdom to tell the direction of victory of freedom and the nip. It nips with dr. Green if you aren't gifted with wine. A rose must be snipped not nipped to be placed in a glass vase. Whether love lives or dies depends on the rose's quality and budding gifted grace.

CUT INSTEAD OF COPIED

*M*aria help me get the snakes out of my ankles then you can like me for me liking you. And when you come to me and lay within a breaths distance, the air I breathe shall become smooth as the control I have to turn glass smooth, water calm, and with the Will to turn ripple air to diamond forsaking a Y*'s in the skies of undulating unending rapids of essence for a prior peace of unknown because too young awe. Laying in the universe of the deserts night with only a tent less rain of a kingdom before there are brothers and families and the entwining snakes of bondage they bring, it is apparent that time has come. Say in that time before a mask for a face there were illusions of other romances of the heart that let my mind my essence of unending rivulets of breath dream bend over backwards breaking the chain of virgin thought in my neck, vibrating to the face of the universe. This at my age and practice has been exonerated as the unsettling of the universe and inside motion cut instead of copied. Thus a boy with potential for rule with the legions in a universal desert night founded in his sinus founded lastly in his mask found his answer to go through time from the beginning to the end of love of eternal undulating rapids or truth of heart and air held smooth breathing time premature diamond till love of eternity enforced, cut till masked of awe to holy god dam authority gave maturity to his lifespan. Maria says through the wall " I will not marry you but I will be your friend." And the raven next door knows this is intended for her and shouts through three lots "You are so old I hope you die" and that is how I feel barely scooping life in the morning and a beta internet particle from a cereal bowl. This feels of no justice, a downward spiral to my heart, an adverse butt inski Rey to fire up a perpetual home of excellent family intentions so I go outside to my car and start the engine and feel the vibrations in my butt and think this is life as much as the raven is of age to know heavy breathing in the heat of the night. Why did I remark that her house unknown to live in and getting remodeled was bang bang bang of nails, bang bang bang on heads, until the Ukrainian committed suicide. I did not know if this was true it felt like it was true at the time of night. It was an act of anger of outrageous misfortune even internationally to the interest in my home: Maria, good people, a beauty of modern appointments, well furnished, a queen bed with just Maria, one room with just myself where a Ukrainian roommate used to be. Well lucky I am and I need the sun the Easter in my eyes just to live. As Margie said " I know He died for our sins." As Freud said " pricks of forced darkness breathing air of paper". "Prudes of mass wear 'em down and tear." And then one morning with a hot dog in my side the raven's and my pet a mother opossum who had seven new born babies clinging to her side came back to her home the home right behind mine. I heard mother nature say "Why do you breathe a pipe and tobacco with an orangutan when the opossum is with fertility and babies?" I did not immediately know. One worker bee called it my Freud. It was a way of self- healing a balance of breathing air and analysis smoothing heart rhythm that could be solace in times of stress. It passes time the weight of light my fire but in the end it leaves no human understanding of bodies perfect like that of the raven hot dogging but passes the wait of pressure.

Caption